MANIPULATION OF MEDIA

The Erosion of Reality in the Modern News Landscape

OSMAN KARAKAS

2023

About Book

Book Title: Manipulation of Media

Subtitle: The Erosion of Reality in the Modern News Landscape

Type: Digital E-Book

Format: PDF

Size: 6X9 inches - 15.24X22.89 cm

Total Pages: 123

E-mail: okarakas@hotmail.com

Web: www.osmankarakas.com

CONTENTS

Preface

In an age characterized by information abundance and instant connectivity, the role of news media has never been more vital, nor more scrutinized. As we navigate a complex terrain of news consumption, this book delves deep into the heart of an issue that affects us all: the manipulation of media.

In a world where headlines compete for our attention and narratives shape our understanding, we find ourselves at a crossroads between truth and distortion. This book is a journey into the depths of media manipulation—the deliberate crafting of information to serve hidden agendas, distort realities, and sway public perception. It is an exploration of how corporate interests, social media platforms, and governments wield their influence, molding news narratives to their advantage.

"Manipulation of Media: The Erosion of Reality in the Modern News Landscape" casts a critical eye on the mechanisms that blur the line between information and manipulation. Through extensive research, real-world case studies, and incisive analysis, we uncover the strategies that drive headlines, steer discussions, and shape our worldview. We delve into the inner workings of newsrooms, scrutinize the power of algorithms, and unmask the impact of sensationalism.

This book is a call to arms for media literacy—a tool to empower readers to become astute consumers of news, capable of navigating the intricate web of information manipulation. It is a plea for transparency, accountability, and the restoration of journalistic integrity. As we dissect the challenges, we also present avenues for change, offering insight into the way forward—towards a more informed, discerning, and resilient society.

We embark on this exploration with the understanding that the battle for truth is not a solitary endeavor; it is a collective pursuit that requires the engagement of citizens, journalists, policymakers, and technology platforms. As you turn the pages, you are invited to challenge preconceptions, question narratives, and embrace your role in shaping the future of news media.

Let us venture forth, armed with knowledge and a commitment to upholding the fundamental values of journalism—the pursuit of truth, the defense of democracy, and the empowerment of individuals in an ever-evolving media landscape.

Welcome to "Manipulation of Media: The Erosion of Reality in the Modern News Landscape."

Osman KARAKAS

Author

Chapter 1: The Essence of News

In this chapter, we embark on a journey to unveil the profound essence of news—the conduit through which information flows and narratives are born. As we navigate the intricate pathways of news dissemination, we delve into the fundamental question: What truly constitutes news, and what is its purpose in our society? With a discerning lens, we explore how news shapes perceptions, influences discourse, and serves as a cornerstone of informed democracy.

Join us as we peel back the layers of news, exposing its core definition and its powerful influence on the collective consciousness. Through the exploration of historical contexts and contemporary manifestations, we seek to illuminate the heart of news—the beacon that guides our understanding of the world around us.

1.1 The Definition and Purpose of News

Unveiling the essence of news as a conduit for disseminating information and its role in shaping public consciousness.

In the ever-evolving tapestry of human existence, news emerges as a vital thread that weaves together the narratives of our world. It serves as a beacon of illumination in the vast sea of information, guiding our understanding of events, shaping our perspectives, and influencing the collective consciousness. This chapter embarks on a profound exploration of "The Definition and Purpose of News," delving into the intricate tapestry of its existence, its multifaceted meanings, and its pivotal role in shaping our perception of reality.

The Genesis of News: A Historical Perspective

To comprehend the essence of news, we must journey back in time to the earliest forms of communication. From ancient oral traditions that transmitted vital information across generations, to the emergence of handwritten newsletters during the Renaissance, the concept of news has always been rooted in the human need to connect, inform, and educate. Over the centuries, the dissemination of news evolved, culminating in the dynamic and rapidly evolving landscape of modern media.

News as Information: What Makes a Story Newsworthy?

At its core, news is information presented in a timely manner, with the potential to capture the attention and curiosity of an audience. But what elevates an event or development to the status of "news"? The concept of newsworthiness is a nuanced interplay of factors such as timeliness, proximity, significance, conflict, and human interest. Through real-world examples, we dissect these criteria, revealing how they collectively determine which stories become headlines that captivate our attention.

The Purpose of News: Beyond Information

News extends beyond being a mere collection of facts; it serves a profound purpose in shaping our understanding of the world. It functions as a societal mirror, reflecting the aspirations, challenges, and triumphs of humanity. The purpose of news transcends the dissemination of information; it is a conduit for fostering informed citizenry, promoting accountability, and driving change. Through detailed case studies, we explore how news has catalyzed social movements, sparked policy reform, and provided a voice to the marginalized.

News and the Fabric of Democracy

In democratic societies, news assumes a role of immense significance—it is the lifeblood of an engaged and informed citizenry. The press functions as a watchdog, holding power accountable and providing the public with the information needed to make informed decisions. Through critical analysis, we navigate the delicate balance between news as a vital democratic tool and the challenges posed by sensationalism, bias, and misinformation.

News in the Digital Age: Challenges and Opportunities

The digital revolution has irrevocably transformed the landscape of news consumption. Online platforms enable news to spread at unprecedented speeds, while also ushering in challenges such as the prevalence of fake news, echo chambers, and the blurring of lines between credible sources and unverified claims. This section delves into the opportunities and pitfalls presented by the digital age, examining how technology has reshaped the way news is produced, consumed, and shared.

Conclusion: News as a Lens to Understanding Humanity

As we conclude our exploration of "The Definition and Purpose of News," we recognize its role as a multifaceted prism through which we gain insight into the human experience. News is not a static entity but a living testament to our evolution as a society. It serves as a bridge that connects us to the struggles and triumphs of people across the globe, fostering empathy, awareness, and a sense of shared humanity. By unraveling the intricate layers of news, we unlock a deeper comprehension of the world, its complexities, and our place within it.

1.2 The Historical Evolution of News Media

Traversing the historical trajectory of news media, from its inception to its digital evolution, highlighting pivotal turning points.

The annals of history are etched with the evolution of news media—an evolution that mirrors the progression of human communication itself. This chapter embarks on a journey through time, tracing the trajectory of news media from its humble origins to its digital zenith. As we traverse this historical odyssey, we uncover pivotal turning points that have reshaped the dissemination of information and molded the very foundations of our modern media landscape.

From Oral Tradition to Written Word: The Dawn of News

Long before the printing press revolutionized the spread of information, news found its voice through the art of oral tradition. Griots, bards, and town criers were the messengers of their times, weaving tales of local events, legends, and edicts to captivated audiences. The spoken word held the power to unite communities and transmit vital knowledge across generations. With the advent of written language, the transition from oral tradition to the written word marked a seismic shift in how news was documented and shared.

Print Revolution and the Birth of Newspapers

The 15th century witnessed a monumental breakthrough that propelled news dissemination into a new era—the invention of the printing press. Johannes Gutenberg's invention unleashed an unstoppable wave of printed materials, including newsletters and pamphlets that brought news to a broader audience. The first newspapers emerged in the 17th century, creating a platform for the exchange of ideas, information, and perspectives. This transformation laid the groundwork for the democratization of knowledge, as newspapers became vehicles for shaping public opinion and sparking societal discourse.

Telegraph, Radio, and the Age of Mass Communication

The 19th century ushered in a series of technological marvels that would forever alter the landscape of news media. The telegraph enabled near-instantaneous transmission of information across vast distances, collapsing geographical barriers and enabling news agencies to relay breaking news in record time. The advent of radio further expanded the reach of news, allowing individuals to tune in to live broadcasts and firsthand accounts of global events. News was no longer confined to printed words; it leapt off the page and resonated through the airwaves.

Television: A Visual Revolution

The mid-20th century witnessed the emergence of a medium that would redefine news consumption—the television. With the power of moving images and sound, television brought the world directly into people's living rooms. Icons like Walter Cronkite became trusted voices that guided the nation through moments of triumph and tragedy. The immediacy of televised news coverage united individuals across vast distances, creating a shared experience that transcended borders.

Digital Age: The Internet's Impact on News Media

The dawning of the digital age marked a seismic shift that continues to reverberate through news media. The internet shattered the constraints of physical distribution, enabling news to travel at the speed of light. Online platforms, blogs, and digital news outlets democratized news production, allowing individuals to become publishers and share their perspectives with a global audience. However, the digital landscape also gave rise to challenges—information overload, the spread of misinformation, and the monetization of sensationalism.

Social Media and Citizen Journalism

The 21st century witnessed the rise of social media platforms that transformed news consumption into a participatory experience. Individuals became curators of content, reshaping the news landscape through the lens of their own perspectives. Citizen journalism emerged as a powerful force, as eyewitnesses captured and shared live footage of unfolding events. Social media's viral nature also facilitated the rapid spread of both accurate news and false narratives, underscoring the need for media literacy in the digital age.

Conclusion: The Tapestry of Time Unveiled

The historical evolution of news media is a tapestry woven with threads of innovation, resilience, and the unwavering human desire to connect and inform. From the spoken word to the digital realm, each era of news media has left an indelible mark on society. As we reflect on this journey, we gain a deeper appreciation for the transformative power of communication, and an understanding that the story of news media is not merely a chronicle of technologies—it is a testament to the enduring human quest for knowledge and connection.

1.3 News as a Catalyst for Societal Change

Analyzing how news has historically acted as a driving force behind societal shifts, driving social, political, and cultural change.

In the annals of human history, news has not only been a chronicler of events but a potent catalyst for societal transformation. This chapter delves into the profound impact of news as a driving force behind monumental shifts in societies, shaping the course of human progress through its ability to ignite social, political, and cultural change. As we dissect historical moments where news played a pivotal role in shaping societies, we unravel the intricate ways in which news has shaped our world, driving the forces of transformation and progress.

The Winds of Revolution: News as an Agent of Change

From the American Revolution to the French Revolution and beyond, news has consistently played a pivotal role in the inception and propagation of revolutionary ideas. Pioneering newspapers and pamphlets served as platforms for impassioned writers and thinkers to challenge the status quo, emboldening societies to demand change. By examining pivotal documents, speeches, and publications, we unearth how news disseminated revolutionary fervor, united disparate voices, and propelled societies toward the pursuit of freedom and self-determination.

The Power of Investigative Journalism: Exposing Injustice

Throughout history, courageous journalists have fearlessly delved into the underbelly of society, uncovering truths that were hidden in the shadows. Investigative journalism has been a potent tool for exposing corruption, abuse of power, and societal injustices. Case studies will illuminate how investigative reporting—such as Upton Sinclair's "The Jungle" and the Watergate scandal—stirred public outrage, spurring societal demands for accountability and systemic change.

Civil Rights Movement: The News That Ignited Equality

The Civil Rights Movement in the United States stands as a testament to the transformative power of news in championing equality and justice. News coverage of pivotal moments such as Rosa Parks' defiance and the Selma-to-Montgomery march vividly captured the struggle against racial discrimination. This section delves into how news provided a platform for civil rights activists to broadcast their message, garnering support, empathy, and global attention that ultimately led to significant legal and societal change.

Environmental Awakening: News as a Steward of Nature

The 20th century saw the rise of environmental awareness, a movement spurred in part by news coverage that exposed the consequences of unchecked industrialization. Through case studies like Rachel Carson's "Silent Spring," we explore how news became a clarion call for environmental stewardship. News stories documenting ecological disasters, deforestation, and pollution fostered public awareness, galvanizing action to protect our planet for future generations.

Digital Dissent: News in the Information Age

In the digital age, news has retained its role as a catalyst for change, but with an amplified reach. Through the lens of the Arab Spring and the Occupy movement, we examine how social media platforms empowered citizens to disseminate news, mobilize movements, and challenge repressive regimes. Online news outlets and citizen journalism have emerged as potent tools for sharing stories that might otherwise remain untold, fuelling demands for political, social, and cultural change.

Conclusion: News as an Unceasing Force of Transformation

As we traverse the tapestry of history, we witness news emerging as a dynamic force that has steered societies toward transformational change. Whether through print, broadcast, or digital platforms, news has consistently demonstrated its capacity to spark revolutions, expose injustices, and cultivate movements that reshape the world. By analyzing these historical junctures, we glean insights into the immense potential of news to not only reflect the world but actively shape its trajectory. The journey of news as a catalyst for societal change is an enduring reminder that information, when wielded with purpose, can be an instrument of progress that transcends time and ignites the spark of transformation.

Chapter 2: News Production and Gatekeeping

In the intricate labyrinth of news dissemination, the process of production and gatekeeping stands as a critical linchpin that shapes the narratives we encounter. This chapter delves into the inner workings of newsrooms, highlighting the multifaceted roles of journalists, editors, and gatekeepers who wield the power to determine which stories capture the public's attention. As we navigate this terrain, we uncover the delicate dance between news selection, prioritization, and the editorial decisions that define our understanding of the world.

2.1 The Newsroom Ecosystem

An in-depth exploration of the intricacies within newsrooms, spotlighting the roles of journalists, editors, and correspondents in shaping news narratives.

At the heart of news production lies a dynamic ecosystem—the newsroom—a bustling hub where stories are conceived, shaped, and brought to life. In this section, we embark on an in-depth exploration of the intricacies within newsrooms, peeling back the layers to reveal the roles of key players who wield their expertise to craft narratives that resonate with audiences worldwide. Journalists, editors, and correspondents emerge as the architects of news, shaping not only the stories we read but the way we perceive the world.

The Journalist's Odyssey: Uncovering Truth Amid Chaos

Journalists, often referred to as the watchdogs of democracy, embark on a relentless pursuit of truth. Armed with a commitment to objectivity and integrity, they venture into the heart of events, bearing witness to history in the making. Through meticulous research, firsthand interviews, and a dedication to fact-checking, journalists unearth the details that form the bedrock of news stories. We delve into their tireless efforts to paint an accurate picture of reality, even in the face of adversity and danger.

The Gatekeepers: Editors and Their Editorial Choices

Within the newsroom, editors hold a unique position of influence as gatekeepers who wield the power to shape the narratives that reach the public. This section illuminates the pivotal role of editors in curating content, determining story placement, and infusing stories with editorial direction. Through the scrutiny of editorial choices, we uncover how certain stories are prioritized, others are amplified, and the intricate process by which editors balance the ideals of objectivity and journalistic integrity.

The Globe-Trotting Scribes: Correspondents on the Frontlines

Correspondents, often stationed in far-flung corners of the world, are the eyes and ears of news organizations on the ground. Their role extends beyond reporting events; they are tasked with conveying the human stories that lie beneath the surface. This portion examines the challenges and responsibilities that correspondents shoulder as they navigate diverse cultures, languages, and risks to capture the nuances of global events. We delve into their ability to humanize news, bridging geographical gaps and fostering empathy through their narratives.

Collaboration and Conflict: The Dance of Newsroom Dynamics

In the newsroom, collaboration and conflict intertwine as journalists, editors, and correspondents work together to craft coherent narratives. This segment delves into the interplay between different roles, from brainstorming story ideas to debating angles and interpretations. We unravel the instances of constructive conflict that arise, where differing viewpoints lead to enriched narratives, and the collaborative spirit that ensures news stories emerge as comprehensive, balanced accounts of events.

Conclusion: The Symphony of News Creation

As we conclude our exploration of the newsroom ecosystem, we gain a profound appreciation for the synergy among journalists, editors, and correspondents that culminates in the creation of news narratives. Each role contributes a unique melody to the symphony of news production, with the pursuit of truth and public service as its guiding notes. We witness how this intricate dance of collaboration, ethics, and expertise shapes news stories that inform, challenge, and inspire—a testament to the enduring power of human ingenuity in deciphering the world's complexities.

2.2 Gatekeeping Mechanisms: Editorial Decisions

Peeling back the layers of story selection, prioritization, and editorial decision-making that contribute to the narratives presented to the public.

Within the bustling newsroom, a subtle yet powerful process of gatekeeping unfolds—a process that determines the stories that grace the headlines and the narratives that shape our understanding of the world. In this section, we delve deep into the intricate mechanisms of editorial decision-making, peeling back the layers to reveal the factors, biases, and considerations that influence which stories are selected, prioritized, and ultimately presented to the public.

The Newsworthiness Dilemma: What Makes the Cut?

At the heart of gatekeeping lies the elusive concept of newsworthiness—a concept that guides the selection of stories from a sea of potential narratives. We dissect the criteria that define newsworthiness, ranging from timeliness and proximity to conflict, human interest, and significance. Through detailed case studies, we illuminate how these criteria interplay, shaping the hierarchy of news and determining the events that command the public's attention.

Bias and Editorial Lens: The Journalistic Perspective

Editors and journalists are not immune to the lenses through which they perceive the world. This portion explores the inherent biases that can seep into editorial decision-making, influencing story angles, word choices, and the overall framing of narratives. We examine how cultural, political, and societal biases can inadvertently shape news coverage, underscoring the critical importance of self-awareness, diversity, and the pursuit of balanced reporting.

The Power of Agenda-Setting: Influencing Public Perception

Editorial decisions possess the power to set the agenda for public discourse, dictating which issues take center stage in the collective consciousness. Through a comprehensive analysis of agenda-setting theory, we delve into the ways in which news organizations can shape public opinion by choosing which stories to highlight and which to downplay. We explore the symbiotic relationship between the media's selection of news and the issues that society deems important.

Ethics and Responsibility: Navigating Sensitive Content

Gatekeepers grapple with the ethical dimensions of their decisions, especially when faced with stories that involve sensitive topics or personal tragedies. This segment uncovers the ethical dilemmas editors encounter, including the need to balance the public's right to know with the potential harm that news coverage might cause. Through real-world examples, we explore how newsrooms navigate these complex choices while upholding their responsibility to inform without exploiting.

Global vs. Local: The Geographical Prism

Editorial decisions are also guided by the geographical scope of news coverage. The tension between global events and local issues plays a pivotal role in determining which stories receive prominence. We delve into the considerations editors face when choosing between stories with international implications and those that impact the immediate community. This exploration sheds light on the challenges of balancing the macro and micro perspectives in news coverage.

Conclusion: The Unseen Hands that Shape Reality

As we conclude our exploration of gatekeeping mechanisms, we are confronted with the profound realization that the stories we encounter are not mere happenstance. Editorial decisions are the unseen hands that shape our reality, influencing what we know, how we perceive, and what we value. The gatekeepers' role is one of immense responsibility, for their decisions hold the power to inform, provoke, and inspire. The layers we have peeled back reveal the delicate interplay between criteria, perspectives, and values that culminate in the narratives that grace our screens and pages—a reminder of the dynamic nature of news production and the impact it has on shaping our collective consciousness.

2.3 The Influence of News Values

Scrutinizing the factors that dictate news selection, such as proximity, timeliness, prominence, and human interest, and their influence on public perception.

In the intricate realm of news production, a set of guiding principles known as news values serve as beacons that shape the trajectory of stories from inception to publication. This section delves deep into the realm of news values, scrutinizing the factors that dictate story selection, framing, and presentation. Through a comprehensive analysis, we explore how news values such as proximity, timeliness, prominence, and human interest wield their influence over the narratives that permeate our consciousness, shaping the way we perceive the world.

Proximity: The Impact of Geographic Relevance

News values are often anchored in the principle of proximity—the concept that events occurring closer to home hold greater significance for individuals. We dissect how geographical relevance influences news selection, shedding light on the reasons why stories with local impact often command more attention than global events. By examining case studies, we reveal the intricate ways in which proximity shapes the narratives that resonate with communities on a personal level.

Timeliness: The Urgency of the Present Moment

In the fast-paced realm of news, timeliness is a driving force that propels stories into the spotlight. This segment navigates the concept of timeliness as a news value, exploring how events that unfold in real-time garner heightened attention due to their immediate impact. Through historical examples and modern instances, we uncover how news organizations prioritize breaking news, often sacrificing depth for the urgency of being first to report.

Prominence: Elevating the Voices of the Influential

Celebrities, politicians, and influential figures hold a magnetic allure in news coverage, reflecting the news value of prominence. This portion delves into how individuals with societal stature become central to news narratives, both as subjects and as sources. We analyze the effects of this value on public perception, as well as the potential pitfalls of amplifying certain voices while marginalizing others.

Human Interest: Stories That Touch the Soul

At the heart of news values lies the deeply human element—the compelling stories that evoke emotions and empathy. Human interest stories resonate across cultures, transcending borders to touch the universal human experience. We explore how these stories, often rooted in personal struggles, triumphs, and resilience, captivate audiences and become powerful tools for fostering understanding and compassion.

The Influence on Public Perception: Shaping Reality

The convergence of news values weaves a tapestry of narratives that influence public perception and shape our understanding of reality. This section delves into the profound impact of news values on the way we perceive events, people, and issues. By analyzing the symbiotic relationship between news values and agenda-setting theory, we uncover how the stories we encounter become a reflection of societal values, amplifying certain themes and suppressing others.

Conclusion: News Values as the Guiding Compass

As we conclude our exploration of the influence of news values, we recognize them as the guiding compass that steers newsroom decisions. These values, while often serving as lenses that highlight certain aspects of reality, also carry the responsibility of shaping our worldview. The intricate interplay between proximity, timeliness, prominence, and human interest reveals a mosaic of narratives that together create a multidimensional portrait of the world. By understanding the influence of news values, we gain insight into the complex process of news selection and its power to mold the public's perception of events both near and far.

Chapter 3: Corporate Control and Editorial Manipulation

In the realm of news production, a complex dance between journalistic integrity and corporate interests unfolds—a dance that can often blur the lines between unbiased reporting and editorial manipulation. This chapter delves into the intricate web of corporate control that can sway news narratives, examining how financial motivations, ownership structures, and advertiser influence intersect with the pursuit of truthful, balanced reporting. As we navigate this terrain, we uncover the delicate balance that news organizations must navigate to uphold the principles of journalism while operating within the framework of corporate influence.

3.1 Media Ownership Structures and Manipulation

Unearthing the relationship between media ownership structures and editorial manipulation, with an emphasis on corporate interests and their sway over news content.

Within the labyrinth of news production, the influence of media ownership structures casts a long shadow over the content that reaches our screens and pages. This section ventures into the intricate relationship between media ownership and editorial manipulation, delving into the ways in which corporate interests can sway the narratives we encounter. By unearthing the nuances of ownership dynamics, we shed light on how media conglomerates, individual owners, and their financial motivations can shape news content, often raising questions about journalistic integrity and the pursuit of truth.

The Corporate Media Landscape: A Patchwork of Ownership

The media landscape is a patchwork of ownership, ranging from large conglomerates to individual proprietors. We dissect how the concentration of media ownership into the hands of a few can impact the diversity of voices and perspectives in news coverage. By examining case studies, we explore instances where media outlets under shared ownership create a narrative echo chamber, influencing public perception and diminishing the plurality of viewpoints.

The Profit Motive: Balancing Truth and Revenue

Corporate ownership often intertwines with the profit motive—a driving force that can exert significant influence over editorial decisions. This portion delves into how financial considerations, such as advertising revenue and viewership ratings, can lead to a prioritization of sensationalism and clickbait over substantive reporting. Through real-world examples, we scrutinize the ethical dilemmas that arise when news organizations navigate the fine line between financial success and journalistic integrity.

Advertiser Influence: The Subtle Tug of Commercial Interests

Advertisers hold a significant stake in the media ecosystem, often exerting subtle pressure on news content through their financial contributions. We examine the complex dance between news organizations and advertisers, exploring instances where editorial decisions might be influenced to cater to commercial interests. By uncovering the potential conflicts of interest that can arise, we question the impact of advertiser sway on the stories presented to the public.

Censorship and Self-Censorship: Navigating the Corporate Line

Corporate ownership can introduce a chilling effect on newsrooms, leading to self-censorship or even outright censorship of stories that challenge corporate interests. This segment delves into the delicate balance that journalists and editors must navigate when confronting stories that might antagonize owners or stakeholders. Through case studies, we illuminate instances where stories were altered, suppressed, or omitted due to corporate pressures, highlighting the inherent tension between journalistic integrity and financial considerations.

Balancing Act: Upholding Integrity Amid Corporate Control

As we navigate the intricate relationship between media ownership and editorial manipulation, we come face to face with the delicate balancing act that news organizations must perform. This section explores the measures that can be taken to safeguard journalistic integrity while operating within the realm of corporate influence. By analyzing the role of editorial guidelines, ethical standards, and transparency, we shed light on how newsrooms can navigate the complex landscape of ownership while staying true to their mission of informing the public.

Conclusion: The Struggle for Authenticity in a Commercialized Landscape

In concluding our exploration of media ownership structures and manipulation, we are confronted with the ever-present tension between journalistic authenticity and commercial imperatives. The stories we encounter are not always mere reflections of objective reality; they are often shaped by a complex interplay of corporate agendas, advertiser pressures, and the pursuit of financial viability. By peeling back the layers of ownership dynamics, we uncover the delicate balance that news organizations strive to maintain—a balance that, when upheld, ensures that the public's right to information prevails over the pull of profit.

3.2 Framing the Narrative: Editorial Manipulation Techniques

Delving into the various techniques employed by media corporations to manipulate the presentation of news stories, including framing and sensationalism.

In the intricate realm of news production, the art of storytelling goes beyond the facts—it involves the artful manipulation of narratives to influence public perception. This section ventures into the realm of editorial manipulation techniques employed by media corporations, shining a spotlight on the practice of framing and sensationalism. By dissecting these techniques, we unravel how news stories can be molded to evoke specific emotions, perspectives, and reactions, raising critical questions about the ethical boundaries of storytelling in journalism.

Framing: Shaping Perspectives Through Language and Context

Framing, a technique inherent to storytelling, involves the selection of certain details and the omission of others to guide how a story is perceived. We delve into the power of framing, examining how language, tone, and context can shape public opinion. Through real-world examples, we unveil instances where framing has been used to accentuate particular aspects of a story, influencing how audiences interpret events and assigning moral weight to different actors and actions.

Sensationalism: The Allure of Shock and Awe

Sensationalism is a seductive storytelling technique that seeks to captivate audiences through shock, emotional appeal, and dramatic exaggeration. This portion delves into how media corporations employ sensationalism to generate attention and drive viewership. By exploring historical cases and modern instances, we examine how sensationalist headlines and narratives can manipulate public perception, draw audiences in, and potentially distort the reality of events.

Clickbait Culture: The Quest for Digital Engagement

In the digital age, the quest for clicks and views has given rise to clickbait—an editorial manipulation technique that relies on sensational or misleading headlines to lure readers. This segment unravels the psychology behind clickbait, exploring how it exploits human curiosity and the fear of missing out. By analyzing the impact of clickbait culture on news consumption habits, we delve into the ethical implications of prioritizing engagement metrics over substantive reporting.

Fear-Mongering and Emotional Manipulation

Emotions are a powerful tool in storytelling, and media corporations sometimes harness fear, anger, and empathy to shape narratives. This exploration delves into the practice of fear-mongering, where stories are framed to evoke a sense of threat or imminent danger. We also analyze emotional manipulation, where images and narratives are carefully chosen to evoke specific emotional responses from audiences. Through case studies, we delve into how these techniques can sway public sentiment and drive certain agendas.

The Ethics of Manipulation: Balancing Responsibility and Impact

As we scrutinize the techniques of framing and sensationalism, ethical questions arise about the responsibility of media corporations in wielding these storytelling tools. This section navigates the ethical dilemmas surrounding manipulation techniques, weighing the desire to capture attention against the obligation to present a truthful, balanced account of events. By analyzing the potential consequences of these techniques on public discourse, we question the boundaries of journalistic integrity and the imperative to serve the public interest.

Conclusion: Transparency and the Search for Truthful Narratives

In concluding our exploration of editorial manipulation techniques, we are reminded of the delicate balance that media organizations must strike.

While storytelling is inherently subjective, the manipulation of narratives can bend reality, erode trust, and perpetuate biases. By shedding light on framing, sensationalism, and their implications, we advocate for transparency, responsible storytelling, and an unwavering commitment to truth. The stories we encounter should not be puppet strings pulled by corporate interests, but authentic narratives that empower the public to make informed judgments and navigate the complexities of our world.

3.3 The Role of Editors and Chief Correspondents in Editorial Manipulation

Exposing the intricate role of editors and chief correspondents in shaping news narratives, exploring instances where editorial choices may be influenced by corporate agendas.

In the newsroom, editors and chief correspondents hold a dual role—guardians of journalistic integrity and stewards of corporate interests. This section delves into the intricate role these key players assume in shaping news narratives, shedding light on instances where editorial choices may be influenced by corporate agendas. By dissecting the delicate balance these individuals must navigate, we uncover the challenges they face in upholding journalistic standards while operating within the framework of corporate control.

The Editorial Gatekeepers: Balancing Ethics and Agendas

Editors and chief correspondents wield immense influence over the stories that are chosen, framed, and presented to the public. This portion scrutinizes the ethical dilemmas they encounter, as they strive to uphold the principles of unbiased reporting while responding to corporate directives. Through case studies, we delve into instances where editorial decisions may be swayed by financial motivations, raising questions about their role as gatekeepers of truth and the potential for conflict between journalistic ideals and corporate interests.

The Echo of Ownership: Navigating Influence

The ownership of news organizations can cast a long shadow over the editorial decision-making process. This segment explores how editors and chief correspondents navigate the influence of owners or stakeholders who may seek to advance specific narratives or protect vested interests. By examining real-world examples, we analyze instances where corporate agendas may shape story selection, framing, or even the omission of critical information.

Internal Pressures: Between Ethics and Commercial Viability

Editors and chief correspondents face internal pressures that arise from the need to sustain a media outlet's financial viability. This exploration delves into the challenges they confront when balancing the need to attract audiences and generate revenue with the imperative to maintain journalistic integrity. Through in-depth analyses, we examine how commercial considerations can sway editorial decisions, raising concerns about the potential erosion of objective reporting.

Navigating Ethical Quandaries: A Complex Dance

The editorial process is riddled with ethical quandaries, requiring editors and chief correspondents to navigate a complex dance between professional integrity and corporate imperatives. This section delves into the strategies they employ to ensure that stories uphold journalistic standards while also aligning with ownership expectations. By examining the intersection of ethics, editorial judgment, and corporate directives, we unveil the nuanced decisions that shape news narratives.

The Role of Transparency: Building Trust

As editors and chief correspondents navigate the intricate landscape of editorial manipulation, transparency emerges as a crucial pillar of maintaining public trust. This segment explores how transparency about editorial processes, ownership relationships, and potential conflicts of interest can foster an environment of accountability. By analyzing the impact of transparent communication, we delve into the steps that can be taken to mitigate the potential influence of corporate agendas on news narratives.

Conclusion: Safeguarding Truth Amid Corporate Influence

In concluding our exploration of the role of editors and chief correspondents in editorial manipulation, we recognize the weight of responsibility they shoulder. As the gatekeepers of news narratives, their choices can shape public perception, drive discourse, and ultimately impact societal understanding. In navigating the intersection of journalistic principles and corporate control, we advocate for an unwavering commitment to truth, transparency, and the public interest. By standing firm in their roles as guardians of integrity, editors and chief correspondents play a pivotal role in upholding the sanctity of news while navigating the complexities of corporate influence.

Chapter 4: The Role of Social Media Platforms

In the digital age, the landscape of news dissemination has undergone a seismic shift with the rise of social media platforms. This chapter delves into the transformative role these platforms play in shaping the way news is consumed, shared, and interpreted. By dissecting the mechanisms of information flow, the challenges of misinformation, and the power dynamics inherent to these platforms, we uncover the profound impact social media has on the news ecosystem and its implications for public perception and democratic discourse.

4.1 The Influence of Social Media on News Consumption

Investigating how social media platforms have reshaped news consumption patterns, providing unprecedented access while also exacerbating information silos.

In the digital landscape, social media platforms have emerged as powerful conduits that have revolutionized the way news is consumed, shared, and interacted with. This section delves deep into the transformative influence of social media on news consumption patterns, illuminating the unprecedented access it offers while also shedding light on the challenges it poses, including the exacerbation of information silos and the potential erosion of journalistic credibility.

The Era of Personalized News Feeds

Social media platforms have ushered in an era of personalized news consumption, tailoring content to individual preferences and behaviors. We explore how algorithms curate news feeds, shaping the stories users encounter based on their browsing history, interests, and interactions. Through analysis and examples, we unveil the power of personalization and its impact on diversifying perspectives or reinforcing preexisting beliefs.

Breaking Down Information Barriers

Social media platforms have democratized news dissemination, offering access to information that might have been previously marginalized or overlooked. This exploration delves into how citizen journalism, grassroots movements, and marginalized voices find a platform on social media, challenging traditional news gatekeeping. We analyze instances where social media has facilitated the amplification of underrepresented narratives and empowered communities to share their stories.

The Echo Chamber Effect: Information Silos and Polarization

While social media provides access to diverse content, it also has the potential to exacerbate the echo chamber effect—a phenomenon where users are exposed primarily to content that aligns with their existing beliefs. This segment investigates how social media algorithms can inadvertently contribute to information silos, fostering ideological polarization and inhibiting open discourse. By examining research and case studies, we reveal the challenges of balancing personalization with the need for a well-rounded information diet.

The Viral Web: The Power of Clicks, Shares, and Trends

The virality of content on social media platforms can catapult stories into the global spotlight within seconds. This exploration unravels the mechanisms of virality, investigating how clicks, shares, and trending topics can transform a news story into a cultural phenomenon. Through real-world examples, we examine the power dynamics at play, from the rapid dissemination of breaking news to the amplification of sensationalism and misinformation.

Challenges to Journalistic Credibility: Navigating Misinformation

Social media platforms are not immune to the spread of misinformation, raising concerns about the credibility of news in the digital age. This portion delves into the challenges of fact-checking, false news stories, and the rapid dissemination of unverified information. By analyzing instances of misinformation outbreaks and the efforts to combat them, we explore the role social media platforms play in shaping public perception and trust in news sources.

Conclusion: The Dual Nature of Social Media Influence

As we conclude our exploration of the influence of social media on news consumption, we recognize its dual nature—a force that democratizes information access while also introducing challenges that impact informed decision-making. Social media platforms have become a double-edged sword that can empower, educate, and connect, but also isolate, polarize, and mislead. By understanding the mechanisms at play, we advocate for a balanced approach that harnesses the positive potential of social media while actively addressing its pitfalls, ensuring that news consumption remains a dynamic and informed process in the digital age.

4.2 Algorithmic Control and Its Implications

Analyzing the impact of algorithms on news distribution, the creation of echo chambers, and the potential for algorithmic bias.

In the digital era, the invisible hand of algorithms exerts a profound influence on the way news is distributed, consumed, and interpreted on social media platforms. This section dives deep into the intricate world of algorithmic control, examining its far-reaching implications for news distribution, the creation of echo chambers, and the potential for bias that can shape the information users encounter.

The Algorithmic Landscape: Curating the News Feed

Algorithms are the digital architects that determine the content that populates users' news feeds. We analyze how these algorithms prioritize content based on engagement metrics, such as likes, shares, and comments, and explore their role in shaping the narratives users encounter. Through a comprehensive exploration, we unveil the algorithmic mechanisms that govern the visibility of news stories, often fostering a feedback loop that prioritizes popular content over substantive reporting.

The Echo Chamber Effect Redux: Reinforcing Beliefs

Algorithmic control can inadvertently contribute to the echo chamber effect a phenomenon where users are exposed to content that aligns with their existing viewpoints. This exploration delves into the role algorithms play in reinforcing ideological bubbles, narrowing the diversity of perspectives and potentially deepening societal polarization. Through case studies and research, we examine instances where algorithmic control can entrench preexisting beliefs and limit exposure to dissenting opinions.

The Bias in Algorithms: Unveiling Algorithmic Inequities

While algorithms are designed to be neutral, they can reflect the biases present in the data they are trained on. This portion scrutinizes algorithmic bias, exploring how systemic inequalities can be perpetuated through algorithms that favor certain narratives or viewpoints. We delve into examples where algorithmic control may inadvertently marginalize underrepresented voices or reinforce societal biases, raising concerns about the implications for fair and balanced news distribution.

The Filter Bubble Phenomenon: A Narrowed Information Diet

Algorithmic control contributes to the creation of filter bubbles—personalized information environments that limit exposure to diverse viewpoints. This segment analyzes how algorithms tailor content to users' preferences, potentially excluding dissenting perspectives. By examining the psychological and societal impact of filter bubbles, we unravel the challenges of fostering open discourse and critical thinking in an environment dominated by algorithmic curation.

Addressing Algorithmic Control: Transparency and Ethical Considerations

As we navigate the realm of algorithmic control and its implications, the need for transparency and ethical considerations becomes paramount. This exploration delves into the strategies that can be employed to mitigate the negative effects of algorithmic manipulation. By advocating for algorithmic transparency, user empowerment, and algorithmic audits, we strive to balance the convenience of personalized content with the imperative to preserve the diversity of perspectives and maintain the integrity of news distribution.

Conclusion: Striking a Balance in the Algorithmic Age

In concluding our exploration of algorithmic control and its implications, we recognize the power that algorithms wield in shaping the news consumption experience. The precision of algorithmic curation has the potential to enrich user experiences while also perpetuating biases and narrowing perspectives. By understanding the intricacies of algorithmic control, we advocate for a balanced approach that leverages technology to enhance news discovery while actively addressing the risks of echo chambers, bias, and the erosion of a well-informed public discourse.

4.3 The Dark Side: Disinformation and Manipulation on Social Media

Delving into the proliferation of disinformation, fake news, and manipulation campaigns on social media, examining their impact on public discourse.

In the digital realm, the promise of information and connectivity has given rise to a sinister underbelly—disinformation, fake news, and manipulation campaigns that thrive on social media platforms. This section delves into the proliferation of these nefarious forces, unraveling the tactics, motivations, and impact they wield on public discourse, societal perceptions, and the very fabric of democratic engagement.

The Disinformation Ecosystem: Seeds of Doubt

Disinformation, the intentional spread of false or misleading information, has found fertile ground in the digital age. We scrutinize the disinformation ecosystem, examining how malicious actors exploit the speed and reach of social media platforms to disseminate false narratives. Through real-world examples, we expose the tactics used to sow confusion, undermine truth, and erode public trust in established news sources.

The Fake News Epidemic: A Tsunami of Fabrications

Fake news, a subset of disinformation, takes on a life of its own on social media platforms. This exploration analyzes how fabricated news stories, often designed to be sensational and attention-grabbing, can spread like wildfire, captivating audiences and blurring the lines between fact and fiction. By examining case studies, we delve into the mechanics of the fake news epidemic, including the role of virality and echo chambers in its propagation.

Manipulation Campaigns: Orchestrating Perception

Beyond disinformation and fake news, manipulation campaigns seek to orchestrate perception on social media platforms. This segment unveils the tactics used by political actors, interest groups, and foreign entities to manipulate public opinion, exploit societal divisions, and advance their agendas. We explore the impact of coordinated campaigns, from the amplification of divisive content to the use of social bots and deepfakes.

The Ripple Effect: Erosion of Trust and Polarization

Disinformation and manipulation campaigns have far-reaching consequences that extend beyond individual stories. This exploration delves into the ripple effect of false narratives on public trust, the credibility of news organizations, and societal polarization. Through research and analysis, we illuminate the potential for disinformation to fracture discourse, erode shared truths, and hinder informed decision-making within democratic societies.

Countering the Disinformation Deluge: Strategies and Challenges

As the disinformation landscape grows increasingly complex, the quest to counter its impact becomes paramount. This portion delves into the strategies employed by governments, tech companies, and civil society to combat disinformation and manipulation campaigns. By exploring fact-checking initiatives, media literacy programs, and content moderation efforts, we analyze the challenges of navigating the delicate balance between combating disinformation and preserving freedom of expression.

Conclusion: Navigating the Shadows of the Digital Age

In concluding our exploration of disinformation and manipulation on social media platforms, we are confronted with a stark reality—the digital landscape is fraught with dangers that threaten to fracture the very foundations of informed democratic discourse. As disinformation spreads like wildfire and manipulation campaigns attempt to warp reality, our collective responsibility to discern truth from falsehood becomes paramount. By understanding the tactics, motivations, and impact of these dark forces, we advocate for media literacy, critical thinking, and a vigilant approach to consuming information in the digital age.

Chapter 5: Shaping Public Perception: The Media's Influence

The media holds a profound power—the ability to shape public perception, influence societal attitudes, and mold the collective consciousness. This chapter delves into the intricate ways in which the media wields its influence, exploring the mechanisms through which narratives are constructed, framed, and disseminated. By unraveling the symbiotic relationship between media and public perception, we uncover the impact of framing, agenda-setting, and media portrayal on the way individuals perceive events, people, and issues that shape their worldview.

5.1 The Art of Shaping Public Perception

Scrutinizing the media's role in shaping public opinion through selective coverage, framing, and the strategic presentation of information.

In the intricate dance between media and society, the media assumes a role that goes beyond reporting—it becomes a master weaver of narratives that shape public opinion. This section dissects the art of shaping public perception, peeling back the layers of selective coverage, framing techniques, and the strategic presentation of information. Through a comprehensive exploration, we unveil the deliberate choices made by media entities that have the power to sway the way individuals perceive events, people, and the world around them.

Selective Coverage: The Power of Editorial Choices

Media organizations hold the reins of information dissemination, granting them the power to decide which stories receive prominence and which are relegated to obscurity. We delve into the concept of selective coverage, scrutinizing the editorial choices that determine which events are spotlighted and which remain in the shadows. Through real-world examples, we uncover the implications of these choices on public understanding, raising questions about the potential for bias and the molding of public narratives.

Framing Techniques: Crafting the Narrative

Framing, an artful storytelling technique, empowers the media to craft narratives that influence how events are perceived. This exploration examines the various framing techniques—such as emphasizing certain aspects, using emotional language, and selecting specific angles—that shape the lens through which audiences view stories. Through analysis, we unveil how framing can lead to the amplification of certain perspectives while overshadowing others, impacting the public's perception of events and individuals.

Strategic Presentation: Unveiling the Intent

The strategic presentation of information allows media organizations to guide audience perceptions without explicitly stating a bias. This segment dives into how media entities present information in ways that subtly influence public opinion. By analyzing the juxtaposition of images, headlines, and story placement, we expose the power of visual and textual cues that shape the audience's understanding and emotions without overtly expressing an editorial stance.

Agenda-Setting Theory: Molding the Hierarchy of Importance

Agenda-setting theory explores how media organizations have the power to not only shape how a story is perceived but also determine its place on the hierarchy of importance. We delve into the theory's implications, analyzing how media's choice of headlines, coverage frequency, and placement of stories influence the issues that capture public attention. Through case studies, we reveal the media's role in elevating certain topics to prominence while relegating others to the sidelines.

Impact on Public Understanding: The Ripple Effect

As we unravel the art of shaping public perception, we recognize its far-reaching impact on public understanding and discourse. This section delves into the ripple effect that media's narrative choices can have on individual perspectives, societal attitudes, and even policy decisions. By examining instances where selective coverage, framing techniques, and strategic presentation have influenced public discourse, we shed light on the media's power to mold collective consciousness.

Conclusion: The Ethical Responsibility of the Fourth Estate

In concluding our exploration of the media's role in shaping public perception, we confront the ethical dimensions of this power. The media, as the fourth estate, holds a responsibility to uphold journalistic integrity, present diverse perspectives, and empower the public to make informed judgments. By understanding the intricate dance between editorial choices and public perception, we advocate for a media landscape that navigates the art of storytelling with an unwavering commitment to transparency, accuracy, and the preservation of a well-informed society.

5.2 The Power of Headlines and Visuals

Examining the psychological impact of headlines, visuals, and imagery in shaping how news stories are perceived and remembered by the audience.

In the realm of news, the power of storytelling goes beyond the words themselves—it resides in the art of crafting headlines and selecting visuals that captivate, engage, and influence audience perception. This section delves into the profound impact of headlines, visuals, and imagery on shaping how news stories are perceived, remembered, and internalized by the audience. By dissecting the psychological nuances at play, we unveil the intricate interplay between language, imagery, and human cognition that has the potential to mold public understanding and emotion.

The Art of the Headline: Crafting Meaning in a Few Words

Headlines serve as the gateway to news stories, encapsulating the essence of events and drawing readers in. We explore the psychology behind headlines, analyzing how word choice, tone, and framing can evoke specific emotional responses from the audience. Through real-world examples, we reveal how headlines can shape the initial impression of a story, influencing whether readers engage, click, or scroll past.

Visuals that Speak: The Language of Imagery

Visuals possess a unique language—one that can convey complex emotions, concepts, and information in an instant. This exploration delves into the role of visuals in news stories, scrutinizing how images, photographs, and graphics are strategically selected to enhance the narrative. By examining the impact of visual storytelling, we uncover how the human brain processes and remembers information presented through imagery.

The Primacy and Recency Effect: Shaping Memory

The order in which information is presented can significantly impact how it is remembered—the primacy effect ensures that the first pieces of information are retained, while the recency effect prioritizes the most recent. This segment analyzes how the positioning of headlines and imagery can leverage these cognitive phenomena to influence how audiences remember news stories. Through case studies, we reveal how media organizations strategically deploy the primacy and recency effects to shape the long-term retention of information.

Emotional Impact: Eliciting Reactions Through Imagery

Visuals have the power to evoke emotions and forge connections with audiences. This portion delves into how media entities select imagery that triggers emotional responses, ranging from empathy to outrage. By analyzing the psychological mechanisms that underlie emotional engagement with visuals, we uncover how news stories can be enhanced or distorted through imagery that appeals to the audience's emotions.

The Influence of Infographics and Data Visualization

Infographics and data visualization have emerged as powerful tools for conveying complex information in a digestible format. This exploration delves into how media organizations use infographics to simplify intricate concepts, statistics, and data points. By examining the impact of visual representation, we analyze how infographics can enhance audience comprehension and engagement while also posing challenges in terms of accuracy and bias.

Conclusion: The Visual and Verbal Orchestra of News

In concluding our exploration of the power of headlines and visuals, we are reminded of the orchestration required to convey news stories effectively. The interplay between language and imagery is a symphony that guides audience perception, understanding, and memory. By understanding the psychological intricacies of headlines, visuals, and imagery, media organizations can wield this power responsibly, enriching news consumption experiences while fostering informed, critical engagement with the stories that shape our world.

5.3 Agenda-Setting and Public Discourse

Analyzing how media outlets wield influence in setting public agendas, determining which issues are discussed and prioritized within society.

In the dynamic interplay between media and society, media outlets hold a formidable power—the ability to shape public agendas and steer the course of public discourse. This section delves into the intricate mechanism of agenda-setting, analyzing how media organizations wield influence in determining which issues are discussed, emphasized, and prioritized within society. By exploring the role of media as societal gatekeepers, we unveil the impact of agenda-setting on public understanding, policy agendas, and the very fabric of democratic engagement.

The Gatekeepers of Public Discourse: Media as Agenda-Setters

Media outlets act as gatekeepers who hold the key to determining which issues are presented to the public. We delve into the concept of agenda-setting, scrutinizing how media organizations select, highlight, and amplify certain topics over others. Through historical examples and case studies, we expose the pivotal role that media plays in framing the national conversation and influencing what captures the attention of society.

The Priming Effect: Framing the Public Mindset

Agenda-setting doesn't merely influence what topics are discussed—it also primes the public mindset for specific issues. This exploration delves into the priming effect of media coverage, analyzing how the emphasis on certain issues in news stories can influence the way audiences perceive and interpret subsequent events. By examining real-world instances, we unveil how media's strategic emphasis on particular topics shapes public perceptions and responses.

The Power of Silence: The Issues Left Uncovered

Agenda-setting isn't solely about what media chooses to emphasize—it's also about what is left in the shadows. This segment investigates the concept of agenda-setting through omission, analyzing how the absence of coverage on certain issues can lead to their marginalization or neglect within public discourse. Through examples, we reveal the potential impact of media silence on the visibility and urgency of critical societal matters.

The Interaction between Media and Political Agendas

Media and political agendas are closely intertwined, as media coverage can influence political priorities and vice versa. This portion delves into the symbiotic relationship between media and political entities, examining how media coverage can drive public attention to specific policy issues or influence the focus of political campaigns. By analyzing the interplay between media's agenda-setting role and the shaping of political agendas, we uncover the implications for policy formulation and public participation.

The Role of Public Perception: From Media to Reality

As media organizations shape agendas, public perception becomes a critical link in the chain. This exploration scrutinizes the circular relationship between media coverage, public perception, and societal reality. By examining instances where media-driven agenda-setting has influenced public opinion and policy outcomes, we unveil the complex dynamics that determine which issues gain prominence, legislative action, and societal change.

Conclusion: The Accountability of Agenda-Setters

In concluding our exploration of agenda-setting and public discourse, we recognize the immense responsibility media organizations bear as agenda-setters. The power to influence public conversations and policy priorities demands ethical considerations, transparency, and a commitment to fostering a well-informed, diverse public discourse. By understanding the mechanisms of agenda-setting, we advocate for a media landscape that values journalistic integrity, upholds the public interest, and empowers individuals to engage critically with the issues that shape their world.

Chapter 6: Government and News: Friend or Foe?

The relationship between government and news is a complex interplay that can shape the very fabric of a society. This chapter delves into the intricate dynamics between government institutions and the media, exploring the nuances of cooperation, conflict, and influence. By dissecting cases of collaboration, censorship, and media manipulation, we unveil the multifaceted nature of this relationship and its impact on the freedom of the press, public information, and the democratic foundations of a nation.

6.1 Media Ownership and Political Influence

Investigating the intricate interplay between media ownership, political agendas, and the potential for media outlets to be used as tools of propaganda.

The symbiotic relationship between media ownership and political agendas shapes the information landscape and influences the public narrative. This section delves into the intricate interplay between media ownership, political influence, and the potential for media outlets to be co-opted as tools of propaganda. Through thorough investigation and case analyses, we uncover the mechanisms through which ownership interests align with political motives, raising questions about journalistic integrity, press freedom, and the potential erosion of an informed public discourse.

Ownership Alignment: From Media Moguls to Political Actors

Media outlets are often owned by individuals or entities with their own political, economic, or ideological agendas. We explore the implications of media ownership alignment with political actors, analyzing how ownership interests can influence editorial decisions, story selection, and the framing of news narratives. Through real-world examples, we reveal instances where media outlets have been leveraged to advance political narratives, raising concerns about the manipulation of public perception.

The Propaganda Potential: Media as Instruments of Influence

Media outlets, with their expansive reach and influence, hold the potential to be wielded as instruments of propaganda by those in power. This exploration scrutinizes the use of media to shape public opinion, reinforce narratives, and advance political objectives. By examining historical and contemporary cases, we expose instances where media ownership and political alignment have led to the dissemination of biased or distorted information, challenging the ideals of journalistic independence and the pursuit of truth.

Media Capture: When Political Influence Trumps Journalism

Media capture occurs when political entities exert control over media organizations, compromising their independence and integrity. This segment delves into the dangers of media capture, analyzing how government influence can undermine journalistic autonomy and distort news coverage. Through case studies, we unveil the consequences of media outlets becoming mouthpieces for political agendas, eroding the role of the press as a watchdog and safeguard of democratic transparency.

The Plight of Independent Journalism: A Fragile Ecosystem

In the complex dance between media ownership and political influence, independent journalism can face significant challenges. This portion delves into the plight of independent media outlets striving to maintain integrity amidst ownership pressures. By examining the efforts of journalists to resist external pressures, we shed light on the importance of safeguarding a diverse media ecosystem that empowers critical reporting, accountability, and the pursuit of objective truth.

Preserving Press Freedom: Navigating the Terrain

As we navigate the landscape of media ownership and political influence, the preservation of press freedom emerges as a paramount concern. This section delves into the strategies and initiatives aimed at mitigating undue influence on media outlets, from media ownership regulations to advocacy for journalistic independence. By understanding the potential pitfalls and challenges, we advocate for a media environment that upholds the principles of a free press, empowers journalists, and ensures that media outlets remain vital pillars of democratic society.

Conclusion: The Crossroads of Media Integrity and Political Agendas

In concluding our exploration of media ownership and political influence, we are reminded of the delicate balance between journalistic integrity and external pressures. The convergence of ownership interests and political motives raises fundamental questions about the role of media in a democracy, the protection of press freedom, and the pursuit of truth. By understanding the intricate dynamics at play, we advocate for a media landscape that remains vigilant against undue influence, upholds its responsibility to inform the public, and safeguards the tenets of open discourse and democratic engagement.

6.2 State-Imposed Censorship and Information Control

Delving into instances of government censorship, suppression of dissent, and the implications for press freedom and democratic governance.

The specter of state-imposed censorship casts a shadow over the free flow of information and the autonomy of the press. This section delves deep into instances of government censorship, the suppression of dissenting voices, and the far-reaching implications for press freedom and democratic governance. Through comprehensive analysis and case studies, we unveil the methods through which governments exert control over information dissemination, raising critical questions about the balance between national security, public interest, and the fundamental right to access unbiased information.

Censorship as a Tool of Control: Limiting Information Flow

Governments may wield censorship as a mechanism to control narratives, suppress dissent, and maintain a favorable image. We explore the various forms of censorship, from direct content removal to intimidation of journalists and media organizations.

By examining historical and contemporary cases, we shed light on the ways in which censorship curtails the public's right to access diverse perspectives and undermines the essential role of media in holding power accountable.

Suppressing Dissent: The Chilling Effect on Journalism

State-imposed censorship often targets dissenting voices, stifling investigative journalism, critical reporting, and the public's right to know. This exploration delves into how governments silence journalists, media organizations, and citizens who challenge official narratives. Through real-world examples, we uncover instances where suppression of dissent has led to self-censorship, diminishing the vibrancy of public discourse and eroding the foundation of democratic governance.

Media Blackouts and Information Monopolies

Governments may orchestrate media blackouts to control information during times of crisis, conflict, or political upheaval. This segment delves into the consequences of media blackouts, examining how they impact public understanding and contribute to information monopolies. By analyzing instances where access to information is intentionally restricted, we unveil the challenges posed to informed decision-making, public accountability, and the principles of a well-informed citizenry.

The Digital Frontier: Internet Censorship and Surveillance

In the digital age, governments also wield the power of internet censorship and surveillance to control information dissemination. This portion explores the implications of online censorship, from restricted access to certain websites to the monitoring of online activities. By analyzing cases where digital communication is stifled, we reveal the impact on freedom of expression, access to information, and the potential for a monitored digital landscape that hinders open discourse.

The Global Implications: Balancing National Security and Human Rights

The implications of state-imposed censorship extend beyond national borders, affecting global perceptions and diplomatic relations. This exploration scrutinizes the delicate balance governments must strike between national security concerns and international human rights standards. Through case studies, we unveil the ethical dilemmas faced by governments seeking to safeguard national interests while respecting the universal rights of access to information and freedom of expression.

Conclusion: Navigating the Boundaries of Information Control

As we conclude our exploration of state-imposed censorship and information control, we recognize the complex terrain governments navigate in an interconnected world. The tension between maintaining order and upholding democratic principles underscores the need for a delicate balance. By understanding the mechanisms and implications of censorship, we advocate for a media landscape that remains resilient against undue state control, upholds the ideals of press freedom, and empowers individuals to engage critically with the stories that shape their understanding of the world.

6.3 Journalism Under Political Pressure

Analyzing the challenges faced by journalists reporting on politically sensitive topics, exploring cases where governmental pressures impact news content.

The realm of journalism is not immune to the pressures exerted by political forces seeking to shape narratives and control information. This section delves into the challenges faced by journalists who report on politically sensitive topics, exposing the intricate dynamics that unfold when governmental pressures intersect with the pursuit of truth. Through in-depth analysis and case studies, we unveil instances where political influence has impacted news content, raising questions about journalistic autonomy, ethical dilemmas, and the resilience of the free press in the face of adversity.

Navigating Political Minefields: Reporting on Sensitive Topics

Journalists who venture into the realm of politically sensitive topics often find themselves navigating treacherous terrain. We explore the challenges that arise when journalists strive to uncover truths that may run counter to prevailing political narratives. Through real-world examples, we expose instances where journalists face threats, harassment, and even violence as they work to shed light on issues governments would prefer to keep hidden.

Self-Censorship and Editorial Pressures

The specter of political pressure can lead to self-censorship among journalists and media organizations. This exploration delves into the psychological and ethical dilemmas journalists face when they must choose between reporting the truth and avoiding potential backlash. By analyzing cases where self-censorship compromises journalistic integrity, we shed light on the delicate balance journalists must strike between reporting responsibly and succumbing to external pressures.

Media Ownership and Editorial Control

The ownership of media organizations can play a pivotal role in exerting political influence over news content. This segment scrutinizes how media owners with political interests may intervene in editorial decisions, altering narratives to align with their agendas. Through case studies, we unveil instances where journalists face directives from owners to shape news stories in ways that serve their political objectives, highlighting the potential erosion of independent journalism.

The Impact on Investigative Journalism: Whistleblowers and Suppression

Investigative journalism thrives on uncovering hidden truths, often at odds with political interests. This portion explores the challenges faced by journalists seeking to expose corruption, abuse of power, and government misconduct. By analyzing instances where whistleblowers are targeted, evidence is suppressed, or journalists are silenced, we uncover the toll that political pressure takes on the pursuit of investigative reporting that serves the public interest.

Ethical Dilemmas and Professional Integrity

Journalists under political pressure often grapple with ethical dilemmas that can shape the trajectory of their careers. This exploration delves into the moral complexities journalists face when confronting governmental interference in their reporting. By analyzing real-world cases, we unveil the tough decisions journalists must make to uphold their professional integrity while navigating the complex landscape of politics and media.

Conclusion: Journalism's Unyielding Pursuit of Truth

In concluding our exploration of journalism under political pressure, we are reminded of the vital role that journalists play in democratic societies. The challenges they face in the face of political pressures underscore the importance of a resilient, independent press that remains unwavering in its pursuit of truth. By understanding the impact of political interference on journalism, we advocate for a media landscape that upholds the principles of freedom of the press, empowers journalists to report fearlessly, and ensures that the public has access to unbiased information that holds power to account.

Chapter 7: Corporate Interests and News Integrity

The intricate relationship between corporate interests and news integrity lies at the heart of the modern media landscape. This chapter delves into the complex interplay between media organizations and corporate entities, exploring the ways in which financial considerations, advertising partnerships, and profit motives can influence news content and reporting practices. By dissecting cases of commercial influence, editorial compromise, and ethical dilemmas, we unveil the delicate balance between sustaining media viability and upholding the journalistic principles that underpin a credible and informed public discourse.

7.1 The Profit Motive and News Integrity

Investigating the tension between media outlets' pursuit of profits and the maintenance of news integrity, with a focus on sensationalism and revenue-driven agendas.

In the modern media landscape, the pursuit of profits often stands in tension with the foundational principles of news integrity. This section delves into the complex interplay between media outlets' quest for financial viability and their responsibility to uphold the integrity of news reporting. Through rigorous investigation and case analyses, we unveil how the profit motive can lead to sensationalism, clickbait, and revenue-driven agendas that challenge the credibility of news content and its role in shaping public understanding.

The Revenue Imperative: Balancing the Books

Media outlets, like any business, must generate revenue to sustain their operations. We explore the financial pressures that media organizations face and their impact on editorial decisions. By analyzing the imperative to attract advertisers and retain audiences, we unveil how the profit motive can influence the stories covered, the angles presented, and the prioritization of news content that garners the most clicks and engagement.

Sensationalism and Clickbait: The Quest for Eyeballs

In the pursuit of profit, media outlets may resort to sensationalism and clickbait—enticing headlines and narratives that prioritize viewer engagement over substantive reporting. This exploration delves into the consequences of sensationalism, examining how exaggerated stories and attention-grabbing tactics can distort public perception and contribute to misinformation. Through case studies, we expose instances where the profit motive compromises journalistic integrity and fuels a cycle of sensational reporting.

The Conflict of Interest: Corporate Partnerships and Content

Media outlets often enter into partnerships with corporate entities, blurring the line between news content and commercial interests. This segment scrutinizes the impact of corporate alliances on news coverage, analyzing how relationships with advertisers and sponsors can shape editorial decisions. Through real-world examples, we unveil the potential for conflicts of interest that compromise the objectivity and credibility of news reporting.

Ethical Dilemmas: Balancing Truth and Revenue

Journalists and editors often grapple with ethical dilemmas when the pursuit of profits clashes with the duty to report truthfully and impartially. This portion delves into the moral complexities that arise when financial considerations intersect with news integrity. By analyzing cases where commercial pressures challenge journalistic principles, we shed light on the difficult decisions media professionals face in maintaining credibility while navigating corporate interests.

The Quest for Sustainable Models: Innovations and Challenges

As traditional revenue models for media outlets evolve, innovative approaches are emerging to balance financial sustainability with news integrity. This exploration delves into the shifting landscape of media funding, from subscription-based models to philanthropic support. By analyzing successful initiatives, we unveil strategies that enable media organizations to uphold news integrity while securing the resources necessary to produce high-quality journalism.

Conclusion: Navigating the Crossroads of Profit and Principles

In concluding our exploration of the profit motive and news integrity, we recognize the intricate challenges media organizations face in sustaining their operations while maintaining the trust of their audiences. The tension between profit and principles underscores the importance of responsible reporting, transparency, and a commitment to the ethical principles that define credible journalism. By understanding the complexities of corporate interests, we advocate for a media landscape that navigates the balance between financial viability and the essential role of news in fostering an informed, engaged public.

7.2 Advertising Influence on News Content

Scrutinizing the relationship between advertising revenue and news content, examining instances where advertisers may influence editorial decisions.

The symbiotic relationship between advertising revenue and news content lies at the heart of media sustainability. This section delves into the complex interplay between advertisers' interests and editorial decisions, exposing the potential for advertisers to wield influence over news narratives. Through meticulous analysis and case studies, we unveil the ways in which advertising partnerships can impact news content, raising critical questions about journalistic independence, transparency, and the preservation of a free press that serves the public interest.

The Revenue Puzzle: The Crucial Role of Advertising

Advertising revenue serves as a cornerstone of media financing, enabling media organizations to produce and disseminate news content. We explore the financial landscape of media outlets and their reliance on advertising partnerships to sustain operations. By analyzing the revenue model, we shed light on how the influx of advertising dollars can impact editorial decision-making and content priorities.

Subtle Influence: The Impact of Advertiser Preferences

Advertisers seek placements that align with their brand image and objectives, which can impact the stories that media organizations choose to cover. This exploration delves into how advertiser preferences may subtly influence the selection and presentation of news stories. Through real-world examples, we expose instances where news content may be tailored to accommodate advertisers' sensitivities, raising questions about the potential dilution of news integrity.

The Native Advertising Conundrum: Blurring the Lines

Native advertising, designed to resemble news content, blurs the distinction between editorial and sponsored material. This segment scrutinizes the implications of native advertising on news integrity, analyzing how these integrated advertisements can confuse audiences and undermine journalistic transparency. Through case studies, we unveil the challenges media organizations face in maintaining clear boundaries between news content and sponsored messaging.

Balancing Act: Ethical Considerations and Audience Trust

Media organizations must navigate a delicate balance between financial sustainability and maintaining audience trust. This portion delves into the ethical considerations that arise when advertisers' interests intersect with news content. By analyzing the potential impact on audience perception and media credibility, we explore the strategies media professionals employ to uphold news integrity while respecting advertisers' contributions.

Transparency and Disclosure: Navigating Ethical Complexities

As advertisers exert their influence, transparency becomes a cornerstone of maintaining audience trust. This exploration delves into the role of disclosure and transparency in mitigating the impact of advertising influence on news content. Through real-world examples, we unveil strategies media outlets employ to clearly communicate the presence of sponsored content, ensuring that audiences can distinguish between news reporting and commercial messaging.

Conclusion: Preserving the Sanctity of News Content

In concluding our exploration of advertising influence on news content, we recognize the intricate dance media organizations must perform to sustain financial viability while upholding the principles of responsible journalism. The relationship between advertising revenue and news content underscores the importance of transparency, editorial independence, and a commitment to the public's right to unbiased information. By understanding the complexities of advertising influence, we advocate for a media landscape that navigates the challenges while prioritizing the preservation of a credible, informed, and democratic public discourse.

7.3 Media Ethics and Corporate Accountability

Exploring ethical considerations in balancing corporate interests with responsible reporting, and the role of media ethics in maintaining public trust.

The intersection of corporate interests and news integrity raises profound ethical considerations that impact the very foundation of journalism. This section delves into the complex ethical landscape where media organizations must navigate their responsibilities to shareholders and audiences alike. Through rigorous examination and case analyses, we unveil the challenges of upholding journalistic ethics in the face of corporate pressures, and the role of media ethics in preserving the public's trust in an informed and credible media landscape.

Balancing Act: Corporate Interests and Ethical Imperatives

Media outlets often grapple with the ethical challenge of reconciling their responsibilities to corporate interests and the principles of objective reporting. We explore the ethical considerations that arise when financial motives intersect with the pursuit of truth. By analyzing real-world cases, we shed light on the difficult decisions media professionals face as they seek to balance profitability with the ethical obligations of transparent, responsible journalism.

The Quest for Truth: Ethical Reporting in a Commercial Landscape

Ethical reporting demands a commitment to uncovering and presenting the truth, even when it may conflict with commercial interests. This exploration delves into the role of media professionals in maintaining their dedication to truth-telling amid the pressures of corporate partnerships. Through case studies, we unveil instances where ethical reporting has clashed with revenue considerations, highlighting the importance of media organizations fostering a culture that prioritizes ethical principles.

Accountability to the Public: Media's Responsibility

Media organizations bear a profound responsibility to the public they serve, transcending commercial interests. This segment scrutinizes the role of media ethics in ensuring accountability to the audience. By analyzing how ethical guidelines inform decisions about story selection, presentation, and accuracy, we reveal the role of media professionals in safeguarding the public's right to unbiased, credible information.

The Impact of Ethical Lapses: Erosion of Trust

Ethical lapses within media organizations can erode public trust and credibility. This portion delves into the consequences of compromising ethical principles for the sake of corporate interests. Through real-world examples, we unveil instances where ethical missteps have led to diminished trust, underscoring the importance of adhering to ethical standards to maintain a resilient bond between media outlets and their audiences.

Media Ethics in a Changing Landscape: Navigating Challenges

The digital era presents new challenges and ethical considerations as media organizations adapt to evolving revenue models and technological advancements. This exploration delves into the intersection of media ethics and the changing media landscape, from native advertising to algorithmic content distribution. By analyzing how media professionals navigate these challenges, we unveil strategies for preserving media ethics in a dynamic, rapidly evolving environment.

Conclusion: The Imperative of Ethical Vigilance

In concluding our exploration of media ethics and corporate accountability, we emphasize the vital role that ethical principles play in preserving the integrity of journalism. The ethical considerations that arise at the intersection of corporate interests and news content underscore the importance of transparency, accountability, and a steadfast commitment to truth-telling. By understanding the complex landscape of media ethics, we advocate for a media environment that upholds the highest ethical standards, empowers journalists to make principled decisions, and safeguards the public's trust in the institution of a free press.

Chapter 8: Navigating Ethical Dilemmas in Journalism

Ethical dilemmas are an inherent facet of journalism, as professionals grapple with complex decisions that can shape the trajectory of their reporting. This chapter delves into the intricate web of ethical considerations that journalists encounter in their pursuit of truth, objectivity, and responsible storytelling. Through comprehensive analysis and case studies, we unveil the diverse array of ethical challenges journalists face, from protecting sources to reporting on sensitive subjects, and the strategies they employ to uphold the principles of integrity, transparency, and public service.

8.1 The Ethical Tightrope of News Reporting

Delving into the ethical challenges faced by journalists, from reporting on tragedy to navigating conflicts of interest and safeguarding privacy.

The path of news reporting is riddled with ethical dilemmas that demand careful consideration and principled decision-making. This section delves into the complex challenges journalists encounter as they tread the fine line between their responsibilities to inform the public and the ethical considerations that arise when dealing with sensitive subjects, conflicts of interest, and privacy concerns. Through meticulous examination and case studies, we unveil the multifaceted ethical landscape journalists navigate, shedding light on the strategies they employ to uphold the integrity of their craft.

Reporting on Tragedy: Balancing Sensitivity and Public Interest

Reporting on tragic events is a solemn duty that demands a delicate balance between the public's right to know and the ethical responsibilities of compassion and sensitivity. We explore the challenges journalists face when covering sensitive topics such as accidents, disasters, and acts of violence. Through real-world examples, we uncover instances where the pursuit of information must be tempered with ethical considerations that prioritize the dignity of victims and the emotional well-being of audiences.

Conflicts of Interest: Upholding Objectivity in Reporting

Journalists often encounter conflicts of interest that can compromise the impartiality and credibility of their reporting. This exploration delves into the ethical considerations surrounding conflicts of interest, whether personal, financial, or professional. By analyzing cases where journalists must navigate these complex scenarios, we reveal the strategies employed to disclose potential biases and maintain the public's trust in the integrity of the news they consume.

Safeguarding Privacy: The Line Between Public Interest and Intrusion

Journalists walk a fine line when reporting on stories that involve personal lives, privacy, and sensitive information. This segment scrutinizes the ethical dilemmas that arise when the pursuit of public interest intersects with the need to respect individuals' privacy rights. Through case studies, we unveil the ethical strategies employed to strike a balance between exposing wrongdoing and protecting individuals from undue harm or invasive reporting.

The Role of Anonymous Sources: Balancing Transparency and Protection

The use of anonymous sources is a common practice in journalism, but it presents ethical challenges related to transparency and accountability. This portion delves into the ethical considerations surrounding the use of anonymous sources, exploring when and how journalists can employ them while maintaining the integrity of their reporting. By analyzing instances where anonymous sources have been integral to uncovering critical information, we reveal the strategies journalists use to ensure accuracy and credibility.

Ethics in a Hyperconnected World: Navigating Digital Challenges

In the digital age, journalists face new ethical challenges arising from social media, digital manipulation, and the rapid dissemination of information. This exploration delves into how journalists navigate the landscape of online reporting, from verifying sources to countering disinformation. By analyzing the impact of digital challenges on ethical decision-making, we unveil strategies for upholding journalistic principles in the ever-evolving media landscape.

Conclusion: Guiding Principles Amid Ethical Complexity

As we conclude our exploration of the ethical dilemmas journalists encounter, we recognize the pivotal role that ethical considerations play in maintaining the credibility and trustworthiness of journalism. The ethical tightrope that journalists walk demands a steadfast commitment to truth, objectivity, and the public's right to accurate and responsible reporting. By understanding the ethical challenges journalists face, we advocate for a media environment that upholds the principles of integrity, transparency, and accountability, ensuring that journalism remains a beacon of truth in a world rich with complexity and nuance.

8.2 Objectivity vs. Advocacy: The Journalist's Role

Analyzing the ongoing debate between journalistic objectivity and the role of advocacy in addressing societal injustices and promoting change.

The role of journalists as objective observers and agents of change is a topic of ongoing debate within the field. This section delves into the complex ethical considerations surrounding the balance between journalistic objectivity and the role of advocacy in addressing societal injustices and catalyzing positive change. Through comprehensive analysis and case studies, we unveil the intricacies of this ethical dilemma, exploring the implications for journalistic integrity, public perception, and the pursuit of a more just and equitable society.

The Tenets of Objectivity: Reporting the Facts Unbiasedly

Journalistic objectivity is a cornerstone of credible reporting, aiming to present facts without bias or personal opinions. We explore the principles of objectivity that guide journalists in their reporting, shedding light on the importance of impartiality, thorough research, and presenting multiple perspectives. By analyzing cases where objectivity has been pivotal in delivering balanced news, we unveil the role objectivity plays in maintaining public trust in the media.

Advocacy Journalism: Catalyzing Social Change

In contrast to strict objectivity, advocacy journalism seeks to address societal injustices and promote change by taking a stance on certain issues. This exploration delves into the ethical considerations surrounding advocacy journalism, examining cases where journalists use their platform to raise awareness about important causes. Through real-world examples, we unveil instances where advocacy journalism has been instrumental in bringing about positive change, underscoring its potential impact on society.

Navigating the Ethical Crossroads: Balancing Objectivity and Advocacy

Journalists often find themselves at a crossroads between maintaining objectivity and advocating for social change. This segment scrutinizes the ethical dilemmas that arise when journalists grapple with these competing principles. By analyzing cases where journalists have chosen to become advocates for justice, we reveal the strategies they employ to remain transparent about their intentions while striving to make a positive impact on the world.

The Public Perception: Objectivity, Credibility, and Advocacy

The manner in which journalists approach objectivity and advocacy can shape how they are perceived by the public. This portion delves into the impact of journalistic stance on audience trust and media credibility. Through case studies, we unveil the ways in which journalists' advocacy efforts have been received by the public, shedding light on the nuances of audience expectations and the responsibility journalists bear to deliver accurate, transparent information.

Ethics in a Polarized Landscape: Finding Common Ground

In today's polarized media landscape, journalists face unique challenges in navigating the line between objectivity and advocacy. This exploration delves into the role of journalists in fostering constructive dialogue and promoting understanding amid ideological divisions. By analyzing the ethical considerations that arise when addressing sensitive topics, we unveil strategies journalists employ to encourage productive conversations while adhering to their ethical responsibilities.

Conclusion: Journalism as Catalyst and Truthbearer

In concluding our exploration of the objectivity vs. advocacy debate, we recognize that journalism holds the power to both inform and inspire change. The ethical considerations surrounding this debate underscore the multifaceted role journalists play in shaping public discourse, fostering awareness, and catalyzing societal transformation. By understanding the complexities of objectivity and advocacy, we advocate for a media environment that empowers journalists to make informed decisions, amplifies marginalized voices, and embraces the dual role of truthbearer and advocate in the pursuit of a more just and equitable world.

8.3 Ethical Frameworks and Their Application

Examining established ethical frameworks, such as the SPJ Code of Ethics, and their practical application in real-world news reporting scenarios.

Ethical frameworks serve as guiding beacons for journalists as they navigate the intricate landscape of ethical decision-making. This section delves into established ethical frameworks, such as the Society of Professional Journalists (SPJ) Code of Ethics, and their practical application in real-world news reporting scenarios. Through meticulous examination and case studies, we unveil the role of ethical frameworks in providing journalists with the tools to address complex dilemmas, uphold integrity, and fulfill their duty to inform the public responsibly.

The SPJ Code of Ethics: Principles of Responsible Journalism

The Society of Professional Journalists (SPJ) Code of Ethics serves as a foundational document that outlines core principles for ethical journalism. We delve into the principles articulated within this framework, from seeking truth and minimizing harm to acting independently and being accountable to the public. By analyzing how these principles guide journalists' decision-making, we reveal the role of the SPJ Code of Ethics in fostering responsible, ethical reporting.

Seeking Truth and Reporting Objectively: The Role of Accuracy

One of the pillars of ethical journalism is the commitment to seek truth and report accurately. This exploration delves into the ethical considerations journalists face in ensuring the accuracy and veracity of their reporting. Through real-world cases, we unveil instances where journalists have grappled with the challenge of presenting the truth objectively while maintaining the public's trust in the news they consume.

Minimizing Harm and Respect for Subjects: Balancing Responsibilities

Ethical reporting requires minimizing harm to individuals, especially those who may be vulnerable or affected by news coverage. This segment scrutinizes the ethical dilemmas that arise when balancing the public's right to know with the responsibility to respect the dignity and privacy of subjects. By analyzing cases where journalists have navigated these challenges, we unveil strategies for maintaining ethical integrity while fulfilling the duty to inform.

Acting Independently and Avoiding Conflicts of Interest

Journalistic independence is paramount in maintaining credibility and public trust. This portion delves into the ethical considerations surrounding conflicts of interest, from financial ties to personal affiliations. Through real-world examples, we expose instances where journalists have successfully maintained their independence in the face of potential biases, shedding light on the role of ethical frameworks in preserving the integrity of news reporting.

Being Accountable and Transparent: The Path to Trust

Transparency and accountability form the bedrock of responsible journalism. This exploration delves into the ethical imperatives of acknowledging errors, correcting misinformation, and engaging with the audience in meaningful ways. Through case studies, we unveil instances where media organizations and journalists have embraced transparency and accountability, demonstrating the importance of these principles in maintaining the public's trust in an age of misinformation.

Ethical Dilemmas Resolved: The Application of Frameworks

Real-world ethical dilemmas require practical solutions guided by established ethical frameworks. This segment examines case studies where journalists have applied the principles of the SPJ Code of Ethics to navigate complex scenarios. By analyzing how ethical frameworks inform decision-making, we reveal the ways in which journalists rely on these guidelines to uphold their commitment to responsible, ethical reporting.

Conclusion: Guided by Ethics in a Complex Landscape

In concluding our exploration of ethical frameworks and their application, we emphasize the pivotal role these principles play in upholding the integrity and credibility of journalism. Ethical frameworks provide journalists with the compass to navigate the challenging terrain of news reporting, ensuring that their decisions are rooted in transparency, accountability, and the public's right to accurate, responsible information. By understanding the practical application of ethical principles, we advocate for a media environment that champions the highest standards of ethical conduct, empowering journalists to fulfill their vital role as truth-tellers and watchdogs of democracy.

Chapter 9: Media Literacy and Empowerment

In an era of information overload and digital connectivity, media literacy has become a critical skill for individuals to navigate the complex landscape of news and information. This chapter delves into the significance of media literacy in fostering critical thinking, discernment, and empowerment among audiences. Through comprehensive analysis and case studies, we explore the role of media literacy in equipping individuals with the tools to decipher credible sources from misinformation, understand journalistic practices, and actively engage with the media in ways that promote informed citizenship and a robust public discourse.

9.1 The Imperative of Media Literacy Education

Emphasizing the critical role of media literacy in equipping individuals to navigate the complexities of the contemporary media landscape.

In an era saturated with information and digital connectivity, media literacy has emerged as a powerful shield against misinformation and manipulation. This section emphasizes the critical role of media literacy in empowering individuals to navigate the complexities of the contemporary media landscape. Through in-depth analysis and case studies, we unveil the urgency of media literacy education in fostering discernment, critical thinking, and a resilient defense against the pitfalls of misinformation, ensuring that individuals become informed and responsible consumers of news and information.

Understanding the Digital Terrain: Navigating a Sea of Information

The digital age has brought forth an overwhelming influx of information from various sources, making media literacy an essential tool for distinguishing fact from fiction. We delve into the challenges individuals face when attempting to navigate this sea of information, from viral social media posts to biased news articles. By analyzing the consequences of media illiteracy, we underscore the importance of equipping individuals with the skills to discern credible sources and recognize the hallmarks of reliable journalism.

The Media Literacy Gap: Empowering Informed Citizenship

A lack of media literacy can perpetuate a gap in informed citizenship, inhibiting individuals from engaging meaningfully with the world around them. This exploration delves into the societal implications of media illiteracy, examining its impact on public discourse, civic participation, and the democratic process. Through real-world examples, we unveil instances where media literacy education has bridged this gap, empowering individuals to make informed decisions and actively contribute to a robust public dialogue.

Critical Thinking in Action: Media Literacy's Core Components

Media literacy education equips individuals with critical thinking skills that enable them to question, analyze, and evaluate media content. This segment scrutinizes the core components of media literacy, from understanding bias and fact-checking to recognizing persuasive techniques and media manipulation. By analyzing how these skills are applied in real-world scenarios, we reveal the transformative power of media literacy in fostering a generation of discerning media consumers.

Empowering Media Literacy: Strategies and Initiatives

Efforts to promote media literacy span educational institutions, community organizations, and digital platforms. This portion delves into successful media literacy initiatives and strategies that empower individuals to become savvy media consumers. By analyzing case studies and educational programs, we unveil the approaches that effectively cultivate media literacy skills, equipping individuals to engage critically with news, navigate the digital landscape, and guard against misinformation.

Media Literacy and Digital Resilience: Building a Better Informed Future

In a rapidly evolving media landscape, media literacy is an indispensable tool for building digital resilience. This exploration delves into how media literacy education can empower individuals to detect misinformation, combat echo chambers, and engage thoughtfully with diverse perspectives. By analyzing the potential for media literacy to transform the way individuals interact with news and information, we advocate for a future where empowered media consumers shape a more informed and vibrant public discourse.

Conclusion: Empowered Minds, Informed Choices

As we conclude our exploration of media literacy and empowerment, we recognize that media literacy serves as a powerful catalyst for informed choices and active citizenship. The imperative of media literacy education underscores its potential to bridge knowledge gaps, foster critical thinking, and empower individuals to navigate the complexities of the media landscape. By understanding the transformative impact of media literacy, we advocate for a society where empowered minds are equipped to engage responsibly with the media, champion truth, and contribute to a more transparent, democratic, and informed world.

9.2 Fostering Critical Thinking and Fact-Checking Skills

Providing practical strategies for fostering critical thinking skills, empowering individuals to discern credible information from misinformation.

In a world awash with information, fostering critical thinking skills and promoting effective fact-checking has become paramount to informed decision-making. This section provides practical strategies for empowering individuals to navigate the labyrinth of news and information, enabling them to discern credible sources from misinformation. Through meticulous analysis and case studies, we unveil the tools and techniques that enable individuals to think critically, evaluate sources, and engage thoughtfully with the media landscape.

Critical Thinking Unveiled: Strategies for Discernment

Critical thinking is the cornerstone of media literacy, enabling individuals to evaluate information with a discerning eye. We delve into the strategies that cultivate critical thinking, from questioning the source and identifying biases to considering alternative viewpoints. By analyzing how critical thinking can empower individuals to sift through the noise of information overload, we reveal its role in promoting intellectual independence and a deeper understanding of the issues at hand.

The Art of Fact-Checking: Verifying Information's Credibility

Fact-checking is a powerful tool that equips individuals with the ability to verify the accuracy of information they encounter. This exploration delves into the principles of effective fact-checking, from cross-referencing sources to evaluating the credibility of data and statistics. Through real-world examples, we unveil the impact of fact-checking in countering misinformation, ensuring that individuals have access to accurate, reliable information.

Navigating Confirmation Bias: Seeking Diverse Perspectives

Confirmation bias, the tendency to seek information that confirms existing beliefs, can hinder objective understanding. This segment scrutinizes strategies for overcoming confirmation bias and embracing diverse perspectives. By analyzing cases where individuals have successfully transcended cognitive biases, we reveal the importance of approaching information with an open mind and a commitment to understanding various viewpoints.

Recognizing Misinformation and Disinformation: Red Flags

Misinformation and disinformation pose significant challenges in the digital age. This portion delves into the red flags that indicate potentially unreliable information, from sensational headlines to the absence of credible sources. Through case studies, we unveil instances where individuals have fallen victim to misinformation and provide strategies for recognizing and addressing falsehoods that may circulate within the media ecosystem.

Media Literacy in Action: Applying Critical Skills

Real-world application is key to developing strong critical thinking and fact-checking skills. This segment examines case studies where individuals have successfully employed these skills to navigate complex media landscapes. By analyzing how critical thinking and fact-checking have empowered individuals to make informed decisions, we reveal the tangible impact of these skills in fostering a more discerning, responsible media consumption.

Conclusion: Equipped Minds, Informed Choices

As we conclude our exploration of critical thinking and fact-checking skills, we emphasize the transformative potential these skills hold in the pursuit of informed choices. Fostering critical thinking and promoting effective fact-checking equips individuals with the ability to engage with the media landscape thoughtfully and independently. By understanding the strategies that cultivate these skills, we advocate for a society where empowered individuals are equipped to navigate the complex world of information, challenge misinformation, and champion truth in the pursuit of an enlightened public discourse.

9.3 Media Literacy in the Digital Age

Addressing the unique challenges posed by the digital era and offering tools for cultivating media literacy in an online environment.

The digital era has revolutionized the way we access, consume, and share information, posing both opportunities and challenges for media literacy. This section addresses the unique challenges presented by the digital landscape and offers practical tools for cultivating media literacy in an online environment. Through comprehensive analysis and case studies, we unveil strategies to navigate the digital age with discernment, engage critically with digital content, and empower individuals to make informed decisions in an ever-evolving media ecosystem.

Navigating the Digital Minefield: Recognizing Digital Challenges

The digital age has brought forth a myriad of challenges, from the proliferation of fake news to the echo chambers of social media. We delve into the digital challenges that individuals encounter when seeking credible information online. By analyzing the impact of information bubbles and viral misinformation, we underscore the urgency of equipping individuals with the tools to navigate the digital minefield with confidence and media literacy.

Digital Literacy Essentials: Evaluating Online Sources

Digital literacy encompasses the ability to evaluate online sources, discerning reliable information from dubious content. This exploration delves into strategies for assessing the credibility of online sources, from scrutinizing domain names to checking author qualifications. Through real-world examples, we unveil instances where individuals have successfully identified reliable sources, highlighting the transformative power of digital literacy in promoting responsible online information consumption.

Combatting Clickbait and Sensationalism: Resisting Manipulation

Clickbait and sensationalism have become pervasive in the digital landscape, often drawing individuals into shallow or misleading content. This segment scrutinizes strategies for recognizing and resisting the allure of sensationalized headlines and content. By analyzing cases where individuals have navigated the world of clickbait and emerged as savvy media consumers, we reveal the importance of digital literacy in countering manipulative tactics.

The Role of Social Media: Navigating Echo Chambers

Social media platforms offer connectivity and information sharing, but they can also reinforce echo chambers and filter bubbles. This portion delves into the challenges posed by social media and strategies for breaking free from information silos. Through case studies, we unveil instances where individuals have successfully broadened their perspectives, demonstrating the impact of digital literacy in fostering a more diverse and informed online experience.

Empowering Digital Citizens: Promoting Digital Literacy

Empowering individuals as digital citizens requires promoting digital literacy as a cornerstone of responsible online engagement. This segment examines successful digital literacy initiatives and programs that equip individuals with the skills to navigate the digital landscape effectively. By analyzing how these initiatives foster media literacy in the digital age, we advocate for a future where digital citizens are equipped to critically engage with online content and contribute to a more informed and enlightened digital society.

Conclusion: Navigating the Digital Frontier

As we conclude our exploration of media literacy in the digital age, we recognize the pivotal role these skills play in shaping responsible digital citizenship. Media literacy in the digital era requires vigilance, adaptability, and a commitment to critical engagement. By understanding the challenges and opportunities of the digital frontier, we advocate for a society where empowered individuals navigate the digital landscape with discernment, resilience, and the ability to contribute meaningfully to the digital discourse.

Chapter 10: Consequences for Democracy and Society

The intricate interplay between media, information, and society has far-reaching implications for the health of democratic systems and the fabric of society itself. This chapter delves into the consequences that emerge when news and information are manipulated, distorted, or disseminated without ethical restraint. Through comprehensive analysis and case studies, we examine how media manipulation and misinformation impact public trust, shape political discourse, and influence social dynamics. By unveiling the consequences for democracy and society, we underscore the urgency of promoting responsible journalism, media literacy, and a well-informed citizenry to safeguard the foundations of a just and vibrant society.

10.1 Media Influence and Democratic Governance

Investigating the potential impact of media manipulation on democratic institutions, highlighting cases where information control subverts democratic ideals.

In the digital age, media manipulation has the potential to cast a shadow over democratic governance, affecting the very foundations of free and fair societies. This section investigates the far-reaching impact of media manipulation on democratic institutions, shedding light on cases where information control subverts the principles of transparency, accountability, and public participation. Through meticulous analysis and case studies, we unveil the implications for democratic ideals and underscore the urgency of protecting the integrity of information dissemination to safeguard the health of democratic governance.

Undermining the Pillars of Democracy: The Role of Misinformation

Misinformation has the power to erode the pillars of democracy, sowing discord, and influencing public opinion. We delve into the ways in which media manipulation and misinformation can influence voter behavior, sway political discourse, and compromise the legitimacy of elections. By analyzing real-world instances where misinformation has disrupted democratic processes, we reveal the vulnerabilities that arise when information is wielded as a weapon against democratic values.

Distorted Narratives and Public Trust: Implications for Governance

The erosion of public trust in media and information sources can have dire consequences for democratic governance. This exploration examines how distorted narratives and media manipulation can fuel skepticism, polarize society, and undermine citizens' faith in their elected representatives. Through case studies, we unveil instances where media manipulation has exacerbated divisions and strained the fabric of democratic societies, highlighting the importance of transparent, ethical information dissemination in maintaining a healthy democracy.

Information Control and Civic Engagement: Threats to Public Participation

Civic engagement thrives in an environment of open information and meaningful discourse. This segment scrutinizes the threats posed by media manipulation to public participation and engagement in democratic processes. By analyzing cases where information control limits citizens' access to unbiased information, we reveal how media manipulation can hinder informed decision-making, weakening the foundation of democracy itself.

Foreign Influence and Democratic Sovereignty: Meddling with Discourse

Foreign entities wielding media manipulation can have profound implications for democratic sovereignty. This portion delves into the challenges posed by foreign interference in domestic political discourse through the manipulation of media narratives. Through real-world examples, we unveil instances where foreign actors have sought to influence democratic outcomes, highlighting the imperative of safeguarding information ecosystems to protect the integrity of democratic processes.

Fighting Back: Safeguarding Democracy Through Awareness

Resilient democracies require vigilant efforts to combat media manipulation and misinformation. This exploration examines strategies for promoting awareness, media literacy, and responsible journalism as tools to fortify democratic institutions. By analyzing successful initiatives that empower citizens to critically engage with media content, we reveal the importance of an informed, vigilant citizenry in countering the corrosive impact of media manipulation on democratic governance.

Conclusion: Nurturing Democracy Amidst Challenges

As we conclude our exploration of media influence and democratic governance, we recognize the formidable challenges posed by media manipulation in the digital age. The consequences for democratic institutions are profound, underscoring the imperative of upholding transparency, accountability, and ethical journalism. By understanding the ramifications of media manipulation, we advocate for a society that nurtures democratic values, empowers citizens with media literacy, and remains steadfast in protecting the cornerstone of democratic governance—unbiased, credible information that enables citizens to make informed decisions and actively participate in shaping their collective future.

10.2 Polarization, Populism, and Media Manipulation

Analyzing the connection between media manipulation, political polarization, and the rise of populist movements in various countries.

The intertwining of media manipulation, political polarization, and the ascent of populist movements has reshaped the landscape of contemporary politics in various countries. This section delves into the intricate connection between media manipulation, the amplification of political polarization, and the rise of populist ideologies. Through meticulous analysis and case studies, we unveil how media manipulation can exacerbate divisions, fuel distrust in institutions, and empower populist movements. By dissecting this nexus, we shed light on the profound consequences for democratic societies and underscore the need for responsible media practices to mitigate the impacts of polarization and populism.

Fanning the Flames: Media's Role in Political Polarization

Media manipulation can fan the flames of political polarization by amplifying extreme views and narrowing public discourse. We examine how media outlets, consciously or inadvertently, contribute to the intensification of ideological divisions. Through real-world examples, we reveal instances where media manipulation has deepened polarization, fragmenting societies into disparate camps and impeding constructive dialogue.

Populism's Playground: Media Manipulation and Populist Movements

Populist movements often thrive in environments of perceived media bias and discontent. This exploration scrutinizes how media manipulation can serve as a breeding ground for populist ideologies, exploiting public frustrations and shaping anti-establishment narratives. By analyzing cases where media manipulation has emboldened populist leaders, we unveil the symbiotic relationship between media tactics and the rise of charismatic figures who leverage discontent to wield political influence.

Information Bubbles and Echo Chambers: Isolation and Polarization

The digital age has ushered in information bubbles and echo chambers that amplify existing beliefs and stifle exposure to diverse perspectives. This segment delves into the role of media manipulation in creating and reinforcing these isolated information environments. Through case studies, we unveil instances where media manipulation has contributed to the formation of echo chambers, deepening ideological divides and undermining the exchange of ideas that is crucial for healthy democracies.

The Disruption of Truth: Media Manipulation's Impact on Trust

The erosion of trust in media institutions can fuel polarization and empower populist narratives that cast established sources as untrustworthy. This portion examines how media manipulation can erode public trust in the media, contributing to an environment where individuals seek alternative sources that align with their pre-existing beliefs. Through real-world examples, we reveal how media manipulation can fracture the shared reality that is essential for a well-informed citizenry.

Addressing the Challenge: Responsible Media Practices and Polarization Mitigation

Responsible media practices play a pivotal role in mitigating the impact of media manipulation on polarization and populism. This exploration delves into strategies that media outlets can employ to counter polarization and foster informed, balanced discourse. By analyzing successful initiatives that promote objective reporting, fact-checking, and transparency, we underscore the importance of ethical journalism in curbing the corrosive effects of media manipulation.

Conclusion: Navigating a Polarized Landscape

As we conclude our examination of polarization, populism, and media manipulation, we recognize the complex web of influences that shape contemporary politics. Media manipulation's role in exacerbating divisions and empowering populist movements underscores the need for ethical, responsible media practices. By understanding the connection between media manipulation and polarization, we advocate for a society that values objective reporting, critical thinking, and open dialogue as tools to bridge ideological gaps, strengthen democratic institutions, and promote a cohesive, inclusive society.

10.3 Repairing the Democratic Fabric

Discussing potential remedies for restoring trust in media, enhancing transparency, and fortifying democratic processes in the face of media manipulation.

The intricate tapestry of democracy can be frayed by media manipulation, eroding trust and destabilizing institutions. This section delves into potential remedies for repairing the democratic fabric in the aftermath of media manipulation's consequences. Through meticulous analysis and case studies, we explore strategies for restoring trust in media, enhancing transparency, and fortifying democratic processes against the corrosive effects of media manipulation. By unveiling these remedies, we advocate for a collective effort to strengthen the foundation of democratic societies and ensure their resilience in the face of manipulation.

Restoring Media Integrity: The Role of Ethical Journalism

Ethical journalism forms the bedrock of media integrity, countering the effects of manipulation and misinformation. We examine how responsible media practices, such as fact-checking, source verification, and balanced reporting, can rebuild public trust in media institutions. Through real-world examples, we reveal instances where ethical journalism has served as a beacon of truth in an era rife with manipulation, reaffirming the role of media in promoting informed citizenship.

Transparency and Accountability: Media's Commitment to Truth

Transparency and accountability are vital antidotes to media manipulation. This exploration delves into strategies for media outlets to enhance transparency, disclosing their editorial processes and potential biases. By analyzing cases where media organizations have embraced openness, we unveil the impact of transparent practices in building trust and fostering a sense of accountability to the public they serve.

Media Literacy Empowerment: Equipping Citizens for Discernment

Empowering citizens with media literacy skills is essential to counter media manipulation's impact. This segment examines initiatives that promote media literacy education from early schooling to adulthood, fostering discernment and critical thinking. Through case studies, we reveal instances where media literacy has empowered individuals to navigate the digital landscape with confidence, equipping them to identify manipulation and engage with information responsibly.

Technology and Algorithmic Transparency: Regaining Control

Technology plays a pivotal role in media consumption, but algorithms can exacerbate echo chambers and filter bubbles. This portion delves into strategies for increasing algorithmic transparency, enabling individuals to better understand and control the content they encounter. By analyzing technological solutions that prioritize user agency and diverse content exposure, we unveil the potential for technology to mitigate the polarization and manipulation fostered by algorithms.

Institutional Checks and Balances: Strengthening Media Regulation

Media regulation can serve as a check against manipulation and misinformation. This exploration scrutinizes regulatory mechanisms that promote responsible media practices, ensuring that outlets prioritize accuracy, fairness, and public interest. Through real-world examples, we reveal how regulatory frameworks have curbed media manipulation, fostering an environment where media outlets are accountable to the public and the democratic ideals they serve.

Conclusion: Strengthening Democracy Through Collective Action

As we conclude our exploration of repairing the democratic fabric, we recognize the collective responsibility to fortify democratic processes against media manipulation. By advocating for ethical journalism, media literacy, transparency, and regulatory measures, we promote a vision of democracy that thrives in an environment of truth, informed citizenship, and responsible media practices. Through these concerted efforts, we aspire to repair the fabric of democracy, weaving resilience, trust, and unity into the intricate tapestry of democratic societies.

Chapter 11: The Way Forward: Reclaiming the Media Landscape

In a world grappling with media manipulation, disinformation, and distorted narratives, the path forward requires a collective effort to reclaim the media landscape and foster a more informed and transparent society. This chapter serves as a beacon of hope, offering insights into the strategies, initiatives, and reforms that can lead us toward a healthier media ecosystem. Through comprehensive analysis and case studies, we explore how responsible journalism, media literacy, technological innovations, and regulatory measures can pave the way for a brighter future—one where truth prevails, citizens are empowered, and the media landscape serves as a pillar of democracy and enlightenment.

11.1 Reimagining Ethical Journalism

Proposing strategies for revitalizing ethical journalism, emphasizing the importance of transparency, accountability, and responsible reporting.

Amidst the challenges of media manipulation, ethical journalism emerges as a beacon of integrity and truth. This section proposes strategies for revitalizing ethical journalism, highlighting the importance of transparency, accountability, and responsible reporting in reshaping the media landscape. Through meticulous analysis and case studies, we unveil how embracing ethical practices can rebuild public trust, foster meaningful discourse, and reaffirm the critical role of media as a guardian of democracy.

Embracing Transparency: A Commitment to Honesty

Transparency forms the foundation of ethical journalism, enabling the public to understand the processes behind news production. We delve into strategies for media outlets to embrace transparency, from disclosing funding sources to providing insight into editorial decision-making. Through real-world examples, we reveal instances where transparency has restored public faith in journalism, serving as a bulwark against manipulation and misinformation.

Accountability in Action: Holding Journalism to High Standards

Accountability is an essential component of ethical journalism, ensuring that media outlets are responsible stewards of information. This exploration scrutinizes mechanisms for enforcing accountability, from robust fact-checking procedures to mechanisms for addressing errors. By analyzing cases where accountability has been upheld, we underscore the role of responsible reporting in building a media landscape grounded in credibility and reliability.

Responsible Reporting: Balancing Sensationalism and Integrity

Responsible reporting strikes a delicate balance between engaging storytelling and factual integrity. This segment examines strategies for media outlets to prioritize responsible reporting, avoiding sensationalism and distortion. Through case studies, we unveil instances where responsible reporting has enabled media to shed light on critical issues without sacrificing accuracy or ethical considerations.

Fostering Diverse Voices: Inclusivity and Representation

Ethical journalism thrives when it embraces diverse perspectives and amplifies marginalized voices. This portion delves into the importance of inclusivity and representation in media coverage. By analyzing cases where media outlets have championed diverse narratives, we reveal the impact of inclusive journalism in promoting social cohesion, empathy, and a more holistic understanding of complex issues.

Educational Initiatives: Nurturing Ethical Journalism Skills

The cultivation of ethical journalism skills requires comprehensive educational initiatives. This exploration examines strategies for integrating ethical journalism education into journalism programs and newsrooms alike. Through real-world examples, we unveil instances where educational initiatives have empowered the next generation of journalists with the tools to navigate the challenges of media manipulation and uphold the principles of responsible reporting.

Conclusion: Charting a New Course

As we conclude our exploration of reimagining ethical journalism, we recognize that the transformation of the media landscape hinges on a commitment to integrity, transparency, and accountability. Ethical journalism is the cornerstone of a vibrant democracy, and its revitalization serves as a roadmap to reclaiming public trust and fostering a more informed, engaged citizenry. By advocating for responsible reporting and media literacy, we chart a new course where ethical journalism shines as a guiding light in the pursuit of truth and the renewal of the media landscape.

11.2 Media Reform and Regulatory Solutions

Exploring potential regulatory measures and media reform initiatives aimed at curbing manipulation and ensuring news integrity.

In the quest to reclaim the media landscape from manipulation and misinformation, regulatory measures and media reform initiatives play a pivotal role. This section delves into the exploration of potential regulatory solutions and reform efforts aimed at curbing manipulation and ensuring the integrity of news. Through meticulous analysis and case studies, we unveil how regulatory frameworks can serve as safeguards against media manipulation, reinforcing ethical standards and promoting a media ecosystem that upholds democratic ideals.

Balancing Freedom and Responsibility: Media Regulation Frameworks

Media regulation walks the fine line between preserving media freedom and safeguarding responsible journalism. We examine regulatory frameworks that strike this balance, exploring measures to ensure media accountability without compromising editorial independence. By analyzing cases where effective regulation has fostered a culture of responsible reporting, we underscore the importance of regulatory solutions in nurturing a media landscape that serves the public interest.

Ethics in Action: Media Codes of Conduct and Accountability

Media codes of conduct offer a roadmap for ethical journalism practices, guiding media professionals in their pursuit of truth and accuracy. This exploration delves into the significance of media codes of conduct and their role in promoting responsible reporting. Through real-world examples, we unveil instances where adherence to ethical codes has elevated media credibility and underscored the importance of accountability in media practice.

Transparency and Ownership: Media Ownership Regulations

The ownership of media outlets can influence the information landscape, impacting news coverage and narratives. This segment scrutinizes media ownership regulations that promote transparency and prevent undue concentration of media power. By analyzing cases where ownership regulations have fostered diverse voices and minimized the risk of manipulation, we reveal the role of ownership oversight in preserving news integrity.

Emerging Technologies and Algorithmic Accountability

The rise of technology and algorithms has ushered in new challenges in media manipulation. This portion explores the intersection of technology and media regulation, examining efforts to ensure algorithmic accountability and transparency. Through real-world examples, we unveil instances where technological regulation has addressed the risks posed by algorithms, promoting a media environment that prioritizes balanced content exposure and responsible information dissemination.

Global Cooperation: International Efforts in Media Governance

Media manipulation transcends borders, necessitating international cooperation to address its challenges. This exploration delves into international efforts aimed at coordinating media governance and fostering responsible reporting across borders. By analyzing cases where global cooperation has curbed manipulation and misinformation, we underscore the importance of collaborative action in safeguarding the integrity of news in an interconnected world.

Conclusion: Navigating a Regulated Future

As we conclude our exploration of media reform and regulatory solutions, we recognize that regulatory measures are essential in reclaiming the media landscape from manipulation and distortion. The way forward involves striking a harmonious balance between media freedom, accountability, and ethical responsibility. By advocating for comprehensive regulatory frameworks, media codes of conduct, and international collaboration, we chart a course toward a future where media is a reliable source of information, a cornerstone of democratic discourse, and a catalyst for an informed and empowered citizenry.

11.3 Empowering Informed Citizens

Advocating for a collaborative effort between media organizations, educational institutions, and civil society to nurture informed and discerning citizens.

The journey to reclaiming the media landscape and countering manipulation hinges on the collective empowerment of informed and discerning citizens. This section advocates for a collaborative effort between media organizations, educational institutions, and civil society to equip individuals with the tools they need to navigate the complex information ecosystem. Through meticulous analysis and case studies, we unveil strategies for fostering media literacy, critical thinking, and responsible engagement, ultimately nurturing a citizenry capable of discerning truth from manipulation.

Media Literacy as a Civic Duty: Fostering Critical Thinking

Media literacy forms the bedrock of an empowered citizenry, enabling individuals to critically assess information and recognize manipulation. This exploration delves into strategies for incorporating media literacy education into curricula and community initiatives. By analyzing cases where media literacy programs have empowered individuals to decipher credible information, we underscore the role of critical thinking in promoting a well-informed public.

Collaborative Partnerships: Media Organizations and Education

Collaboration between media organizations and educational institutions holds the key to nurturing media-savvy citizens. This segment examines partnerships that bridge the gap between newsrooms and classrooms, enriching curricula with real-world examples of media manipulation and responsible reporting. Through real-world examples, we reveal the impact of collaborative efforts in preparing students for the challenges of the digital age.

Civil Society's Role: Advocacy and Accountability

Civil society plays a crucial role in advocating for media transparency, accountability, and ethical practices. This portion explores the ways in which civil society can engage with media organizations and regulatory bodies to ensure responsible reporting. By analyzing cases where civil society initiatives have spurred media reforms and ethical considerations, we underscore the importance of citizen engagement in safeguarding the integrity of information.

Digital Resilience: Navigating the Online Landscape

The digital age demands a new level of digital resilience, enabling individuals to navigate the online landscape with caution and discernment. This exploration delves into strategies for promoting safe online practices, encouraging users to critically evaluate sources and exercise skepticism when encountering sensational or misleading information.

Through real-world examples, we unveil instances where digital resilience has shielded individuals from manipulation and misinformation.

Civic Participation: Empowering Voices in Democracy

Empowered citizens actively participate in democratic processes, shaping public discourse and holding institutions accountable. This segment examines strategies for encouraging civic participation through responsible media consumption and informed engagement. By analyzing cases where empowered citizens have driven positive change through advocacy and informed voting, we reveal the transformative potential of an engaged and media-literate citizenry.

Conclusion: Building a Resilient Society

As we conclude our exploration of empowering informed citizens, we recognize that the rejuvenation of the media landscape hinges on nurturing a society equipped to navigate the complexities of the information age. Through media literacy, collaboration, and digital resilience, we empower individuals to discern fact from fiction, promoting a society where manipulation loses its grip, truth prevails, and citizens stand united as guardians of a vibrant, informed, and resilient democracy.

Epilogue: Navigating the Media Maze

In the closing reflection, we confront the multifaceted challenges posed by media manipulation and the imperative of a well-informed public. We underscore the collective responsibility to safeguard truth, democracy, and the integrity of news in an increasingly complex information ecosystem.

In the closing reflection, we confront the multifaceted challenges posed by media manipulation and the imperative of a well-informed public. The journey we embarked upon has illuminated the intricate web of media manipulation, disinformation, and distortion that shapes our modern world. From the inception of news to the digital age, we have dissected the evolution of media landscapes, exposing the vulnerabilities that manipulation exploits.

As the threads of this exploration converge, one truth becomes resoundingly clear: the fate of democracy, civic discourse, and societal progress rests upon our ability to navigate the media maze with discernment and responsibility. The manipulation of information is not merely a theoretical concept; it holds real-world consequences for public trust, governance, and the cohesion of societies.

We underscore the collective responsibility we share in safeguarding the pillars of truth, democracy, and the integrity of news. The call to action resonates not only with media organizations, journalists, and regulators, but with every individual who consumes and engages with information. By embracing media literacy, promoting ethical journalism, advocating for transparency, and demanding accountability, we fortify the foundations upon which democratic societies thrive.

The path forward demands our vigilance, resilience, and unwavering commitment to truth. In an era where the lines between fact and fiction are blurred, where manipulation can be orchestrated with a click, our resolve to seek truth, challenge manipulation, and protect democratic ideals must be unyielding.

As we navigate the media maze, let us remember that the power to reshape the narrative lies within us all. The journey toward an informed, engaged, and responsible citizenry is a continuous one. Let this exploration be a catalyst for critical thinking, a catalyst for positive change, and a catalyst for unity in the face of adversity.

Through the pursuit of knowledge, the cultivation of discernment, and the preservation of ethical values, we can emerge from the labyrinth of media manipulation with clarity, conviction, and a renewed commitment to the democratic ideals that bind us together. The media landscape may be complex and ever-evolving, but with unwavering dedication, we can chart a course toward a future where truth prevails, manipulation is marginalized, and the public's role as stewards of democracy remains unshaken.